# Jerry N. Uelsmann

Twenty-five Years: A Retrospective

1976

# Jerry N. Uelsmann

## Twenty-five Years: A Retrospective

*by James L. Enyeart*

*A New York Graphic Society Book*

Little, Brown and Company · Boston

*First edition*

*New York Graphic Society books
are published by Little, Brown and Company
Published simultaneously in Canada
by Little, Brown and Company (Canada) Limited*

*Printed in the United States of America*

*Library of Congress Cataloging in Publication Data*

Uelsmann, Jerry, 1934–
    Jerry N. Uelsmann, twenty-five years.

    "A New York Graphic Society book."
    Bibliography: p.
    1. Photography, Composite.   2. Uelsmann,
Jerry, 1934–     . I. Enyeart, James.
II. Title.  III. Title: Jerry N. Uelsmann, 25 years.
TR685.U343   1982      779'.092'4      82-12736
ISBN 0-8212-1519-1

# Contents

*For Diane and Andrew*
J. N. U.


*For Roxanne, Mara, Sasha, Megan*
J. L. E.

# Preface

Each rebirth of appreciation of a particular artistic discipline carries with it the discovery of both artists who savor style as a demonstration of aesthetic prowess, and artists who attempt to change our thinking about the art form itself. Jerry Uelsmann is one of the latter. As Peter Bunnell (McAlpin Professor of the History of Photography and Modern Art at Princeton University) noted, Uelsmann "may be seen to have altered the language, the substance, and the direction" of photography itself.[1] While his work is known for its distinctive style, it is also recognized for its effectiveness in expressing his ideas, enigmatic as they may be; his philosophy, which has turned photographic technique on its head; and his humor, poetry, and emotion. Such content separates Uelsmann's photographs from those of photographers who use style as an end in itself. All too often technique is mistaken for style in the larger meaning of the word, and then craft alone receives undue veneration. This essay deals with Uelsmann's technique only to elucidate the evolution of his ideas. Moreover, it traces his development as a major artist without preoccupation with biographical detail or amateur psychoanalysis, since both of these approaches are concerned as much with a kind of societal voyeurism as with art itself.

Uelsmann's photographs, by their figurative nature, invite attempts to describe and discuss them. Yet language is at best but a metaphor for what is experienced through vision. When we describe something we have seen, we compare it with something else. In any form of communication, of course, symbols are used to represent feelings and ideas.

By discussing Uelsmann's work in retrospect, I hope to unravel exactly what his photographic metaphors represent and what the roots of his choice of symbols are. His own words—what he has written in letters and articles and said in interviews—can provide links to a deeper understanding of the evolution of his imagery. However, when Uelsmann is quoted here, his words are often taken out of their chronological frame; the quotation may not come from the period being discussed, but is being studied for its inherent meaning, much as we look at one of his photographs.

I have organized the discussion of Uelsmann's work into three periods: 1954–1966, the early work, which reveals not only influences but nascent aesthetic attitudes; 1967–1975, the period in which he received the most significant critical attention; and 1976–1981, the recent work. Following the text is a portfolio of photographs, also presented in three periods. Although they relate to the respective discussions, the photographs are intended to play an independent role. The selection is exceptional in one regard: for his previous books, Uelsmann was largely responsible for the choice of images reproduced and did not allow significant editing by any other party. It is the nature of artists to want to edit their work for us. It is the means by which they teach us about it, and, after all, they are the primary editors, making the initial choices of what will survive. The selection for this book, however, was made by the author, with Uelsmann's blessing. He remains protective, sometimes argumentative, about individual photographs, but on the whole he is confident that what appears here represents a fair and sympathetic view of his work in retrospect.

In attempting to describe and understand Uelsmann's work, I am conscious that one metaphor (language) cannot thoroughly represent another metaphor (photography). As Goethe writes in *Faust*: "He who wishes to understand or to describe anything, first tries to expel the life. Then he has got the parts in his hand. The only thing lacking is the spiritual bond."[2] I accept the challenge implied, realizing that Uelsmann's photographs are linked directly to the mind; that to describe is to intervene; that what the mind intuits is translated into emotions and feelings without verbal support. I will attempt here, then, to display the "parts" (influences, ideas, motifs, and iconography) and to share with the reader as much as possible the initial inspiration and "spiritual bond" between Uelsmann and his work.

# Introduction

# 1954–1966

Imagine a youth crawling under a carnival tent anticipating a midway show, only to find a Holy Rollers meeting. This is a fair analogy to Jerry Uelsmann's entering the Rochester Institute of Technology in 1953, expecting to study a standard curriculum of visual communication and commercial photography and instead finding Ralph Hattersley and Minor White teaching there. He was saved—but not fully converted until he entered Henry Holmes Smith's "seminary" at Indiana University in 1958. The creative forces of Hattersley and White played no small role in liberating Uelsmann from the leaden weight of convention, but it was the challenges of Henry Holmes Smith, hurling piercing questions about Uelsmann's motivations and philosophy, that directed him as an artist. In a letter to Peter Bunnell in 1974, Uelsmann wrote:

*Henry truly was my most important teacher. . . . While he didn't have the mystery of a Minor, he had enough mental energy to light a city the size of New York for ten years! Henry forced me into deep water. In many ways I was overconfident and a little too damn clever for my own good. He was a constant challenge. He could listen in a way that my naive questions became questions of substance. He could out-"clever" me, and could beat me at all of my own games. I was forced to be real, to think about what I was doing. I must confess that there was the element of pain. I have since learned that most real growth and stretching involves pain. It was an intense catalytic relationship. Henry was high priest at my photographic puberty rites.*

Throughout his years as a student of primarily commercial photography, Uelsmann found success too easily attainable. From the beginning, his inherent craftsmanship provided a slick polish to the design problems placed before him. But his association with these three artist-teachers made that easy success invariably less than satisfying. Through them, he recognized the deeper value of struggling with unresolvable problems. In 1962, finding himself after two years of teaching at the University of Florida in a position similar to that of the mentors of his student years, Uelsmann wrote an appraisal of their influence on him as part of an elaboration of his current thoughts on photography. This was in effect, the draft of his first manifesto and provided the foundation for the articles about his work, including his essays on "post-visualization" and "in-process discovery," that Uelsmann published over the following years. In it he wrote:

*The following three men have been significant influences: Ralph Hattersley, Minor White, Henry Holmes Smith. Hattersley was the first to push me beyond my initial commercial interest in photography. It was he who introduced me to photography for photography's sake. White was the director of the demolition crew that attacked my romantic youthful preconceptions of what I thought photography was and should be. He held back the bushes to indicate possible paths up the mountain. I am most indebted to Henry Holmes Smith. He is a master of the highly calculated, apparently casual remark or gesture. He could offend and he could praise; his sense of timing was exquisite. No other individual has ever made me more upset or happier [than he did] by his always relevant comments.*[3]

As might be expected of any artist's work produced in the captive environment of formal education—however inspiring—Uelsmann's photographs from his student years are eclectic and grounded primarily in subjects common to the masters of the period. Yet, not only are there exceptions within this body of work, but much of it is unusual even when it is dependent on models. There is a maturity of execution and presentation that far exceeds one's expectations of student work. Certainly the photographs benefit from Uelsmann's inherent craftsmanship, but they also show a predilection toward subjects that, even in their great variety, seem larger than life and evoke painfully serious, taut, and half-buried emotions. There can be no question that these works anticipate, both in content and in form, the more complete aberration from earthly reality characteristic of his mature work.

In two of these photographs from 1954 (figures 1, 2), one can recognize early manifestations of an aesthetic based on an intentional convolution of humor, troublesome emotions, and a formal play of two-dimensional space against photography's commanding illusion of three-dimensional space. In one of the photographs, a solemn man peers hesitantly from behind and between two floating shapes of paper that dominate the foreground. All else is reduced to a black background that pushes from behind against the three forms. This playful compression of space in a believable situation is at the very root of Uelsmann's later mastery of multiple imagery. It is a straight photograph, like nearly all of his work before 1961, and does not utilize the technique of multiple printing. The illusion and mystery of the image are the result of manipulating physical objects that are

Figure 1. *1954*

Figure 2. *1954*

not yet symbolic, nor particularly shocking in their juxtaposition. In Uelsmann's later works, these contiguous forms become indefinite symbols, and the spiritual qualities of inanimate objects are anthropomorphized.

A second image from this year is an example of Uelsmann's relationship with surrealism. Although his photographs have the appearance of being surreal, their process of creation is antithetical to the original dogma of Surrealism. The surreal quality derives simply from making the absurd believable (an issue that will be taken up in greater detail later). In the photograph, a rather austere, conventionally dressed man sits in an environment typical of the standard studio portrait: the subject is shown against a mottled, painterly background and the obligatory halo circles his head. But where the sitter's hand should be is a foot—holding a cigarette. Obviously the image was intended as a light satire of such conventional photographs. The photograph is humorous and yet at the same time pathetic. The viewer wants to laugh, but the painfully mournful expression on the man's face disturbs the fragile humor. Again, the image has been achieved without multiple printing. At this point in the evolution of Uelsmann's imagery, his approach is still "realistic" and the viewer knows immediately that the foot is placed in a conspicuous position so that it will look absurd. Nevertheless, the illusion is successful enough to make the viewer want to believe in the absurdity against the logic of the situation. The persuasion of the viewer to believe in the unbelievable is the basis upon which Uelsmann will develop a style wholly his own in subsequent years.

Although his original interest at R I T had been commercial photography, Uelsmann had been shown the way to photography for photography's sake by Hattersley and White. Certainly these photographs reveal that guidance, and the underlying qualities of mystery and metaphor emanating from them Uelsmann directly attributes to White's inspiration:

*When I was a student of Minor White's, he used to have a dictum that went "one should photograph objects, not only for what they are, but for what else they are." We were concerned with the kind of metamorphosis that photography could allow, that while literally a photograph might show a broken balustrade [ figure 3], a fragment of an old building, the shapes themselves were very anthropomorphic, they were very human, there were other qualities that the image had that transcended the literal subject matter.*[4]

Figure 3. *1961 Caryatids*

Between the years 1954 and 1960, Uelsmann's work was stylistically a survey of the straight photography tradition of the 1950s. By 1961, however, his photographs were based in experimental philosophy and technique. While the quality and depth of knowledge Uelsmann gained in this area is most assuredly attributable to Henry Holmes Smith, at least one example from 1955, prior to his association with Smith, suggests a latent predisposition to radical manipulation of accepted photographic imagery (figure 4). This photograph does not have the complexity we now associate with Uelsmann's work, yet it is a first expression of a personal iconography devoted to metaphoric imagery of man and nature; genesis–the seed–birth will become a recurring theme. A female nude, the symbol of fertility, sensuality, and the origin of life itself, seems to stand in the midst of a storm of elements of the kind and force that formed the universe. This early attempt to idealize the nude, however, resulted in a voluptuousness that overshadowed the intended seriousness of the content. Nevertheless, the photograph is one of the earliest successful examples of a technique Uelsmann used to liberate photography and reality from a documentary, slice-of-life mode. Referring to this approach, Uelsmann has said:

*Let us not delude ourselves by the seemingly scientific nature of the darkroom ritual; it has been and always will be a form of alchemy. Our overly precious attitude toward that ritual has tended to conceal from us an innermost world of mystery, enigma, and insight.*[5]

Although these early photographs are limited accomplishments within the total body of his work, they are of considerable interest within the chronological context of his aesthetic development.

The photographs from 1956 to 1961 reproduced in section one represent the best of this period, years in which Uelsmann shows the most varied stylistic concerns of his career and in which his work was dominated by the aesthetic of the straight photograph. In 1962,

Figure 4. *1955*

Figure 6. *1961 Street Singer*

Figure 5. *1956*

his photographs began to manifest a more accomplished, more coherent style based largely
on his perfecting of multiple-printing technique, combined with a radical displacement of
his subjects from their expected orientation. The extreme variety in Uelsmann's work
before 1962 makes it clear that there was no deep or direct influence of any single photographer; his own comments on the making of this book reinforce this point:

*I really never became an apostle of any photographer, even though I was inspired by many.
A little bit of the spirit of all of the silver heroes of the fifties is there. The range is so great,
from pure documentary, to spiritual, to experimental, that you could prove anything. So it
is that I feel the content of the text should influence the selection. Most of the work, because it
is formative, should probably be included in the body of the text and not represented as fine
photographs. (I should add that there are many that I have rediscovered and that I would not
be embarrassed by.) In any case, the point I am trying to make is that if you want to show how*

*a little of Minor caught my heart, or a little Callahan caught my eye, or Sommer caught my mind. It's all there.*[6]

The effect of being inspired by many heroes and emulating their styles was that Uelsmann gained an early understanding of what it means to have an individual aesthetic. It is apparent that from the beginning he found in each the same emotional base in, and appreciation for, classical form that ran through the depths of his own being. A sampling of the photographs showing the most obvious pictorial relationships to the works of other photographers reveals a similarity of subject matter and an underlying empathy in terms of the dramatic, humanistic, and emotional content. Figures 5 and 6, from 1956 and 1961, are straightforward documents that could have been inspired by a mixture of the sensibilities of Walker Evans and the photographers of the Farm Security Administration. Figure 7 owes its subject matter to Aaron Siskind, and the mood of the image echoes Siskind's concerns for portraying what we feel about the world and want it to mean as opposed to what it looks like.[7] Figure 8 recalls Frederick Sommer's mastery in extracting the inherent

Figure 7. *1958*

Figure 8. *1959*

mysterious symbolism of found objects while amplifying that spiritual essence through sensuous lighting and a critically structured composition. A number of images from 1961 reflect the gospel of significant form according to Edward and Brett Weston. In figure 9, Uelsmann has combined what appear to be a nude (actually an arm) and a pepper, perhaps the two most recognizable symbols of Edward Weston's photography. Despite Weston's claim that his pepper photographs had little erotic association, Uelsmann seems to have smiled, along with the majority of viewers, and joined the two subjects in humorous tribute to the master. There is also in this photograph a hint of Uelsmann's obsession with anonymous embryonic forms found in all of nature. Figure 10 echoes the classical tradition of balanced form, but in this case more in the still-life genre of Brett Weston than that of his father. Further evidence of Uelsmann's eclectic interest in the masters of the fifties can be found in the Callahan-like image of figure 11, and the negative tone landscape of figure 12, which is reminiscent of Minor White's works utilizing the infrared technique.

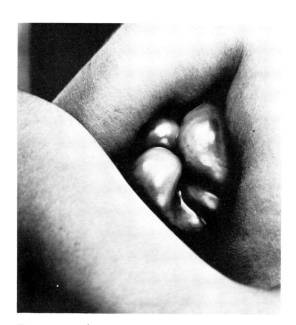

Figure 9. *1961*

Figure 10. *1961*

While these associations help sort out Uelsmann's predilections during a crucial, formative period, such comparisons must be kept in perspective. As Uelsmann said, "the range is so great that you could prove anything." The very fact that he produced works of substantial merit in the style of masters of the period was no mean accomplishment. It is also apparent that all these photographers, including Uelsmann, share an emotional and psychological attitude affirming the mystery of art and life. Each is on record regarding the relationship of their emotions to the aesthetics of their work. Uelsmann has said:

*It seems to me that life abounds with mystery, that it is central to life, that when you are alive there are many kinds of questions . . . and it is the challenge of the questions that makes life exciting.*

*I think of my photographs as being obviously symbolic but not symbolically obvious. There isn't any specific correlation between the symbols in the image and any content that I have in mind.*[8]

Figure 11. *1961*

Figure 12. *1961*

Indeed, the symbolism in Uelsmann's work is generally enigmatic and not easily related to a specific narrative concept. During the late fifties and early sixties, he titled the majority of his photographs; the titles used were haiku-like explanations, or at least they were intended as keys to the symbolism employed. Titles like *Enigmatic Figure*, *Restricted Man*, *Equivalent*, and *Magritte's Touchstone* (figures 13, 14, 15, and 16) are typical in their poetic and philosophical nature. But the titles are often limiting to the work itself and make too obvious a symbolism that, paradoxically, may have more intense possibilities if the work were given a less literary title. For example, in *Equivalent*, a man's hand and a nude female body approximate similarity in form, size, and attitude. The image is made somewhat humorous and satirical by the title, which refers to the term used by Alfred Stieglitz to describe the emotional and philosophical intent of his photographs. If Uels-

Figure 13. *1959 Enigmatic Figure*

Figure 14. *1961 Restricted Man*

Figure 15. *1964 Equivalent*

Figure 16. *1965 Magritte's Touchstone*

mann's photograph were untitled, or the word "equivalent" were without historical reference, appreciation of the two forms might be less lighthearted. Similarly, Uelsmann's titles block viewers from perceiving the uniqueness of his vision. The title *Magritte's Touchstone*, for example, tends to limit appreciation of the photograph in terms of Magritte's personal brand of surrealism. In this instance, the title also misleads the viewer into making too direct a relationship between Uelsmann and the Surrealists. Uelsmann is only mildly surrealist. The relationship is purely visual and not philosophical. Even when the titles are not as directly referential as the two just discussed, the effect is similar. Both "*Enigmatic Figure*" and "*Restricted Man*" guide viewers' perceptions toward a specific interpretation of the curious visions before them. The title *Enigmatic Figure* draws one's attention to the figure and hence to the seedpod that serves as a head. As a result, one feels there is a certain corniness in the construction of the figure. In addition, titling an enigmatic image as "enigmatic" lessens the impact of discovery; it decreases the viewer's desire for participation and interpretation. Untitled, this work would invite a far closer scrutiny of its revelation of an integration between the organic forms of man and nature.

It would be a mistake to be overly serious about this image, however. It is an early work and definitely contains elements of Uelsmann's humor. The seedpod is intrinsically worth a smile, and the knaur on the log positioned in exactly the proper place to represent the penis of the transparent figure is good for more than a smile. Uelsmann's humor is a dominant element in his personality even today, and it has always slipped into his work without warning to the viewer, often in the most unexpected images. Henry Holmes Smith drew attention to this aspect of Uelsmann's work:

*Uelsmann must not be taken seriously always. His sense of humor may be a little "squirmy" and sometimes open to question when one can't quite laugh for the embarrassment it causes, but must be taken into account.*[9]

Uelsmann uses humor in his photographs the way one uses the pun in language, with the double meaning and the often embarrassing oversimplification. But the simplicity of the humor should not be misunderstood, for it is in its nature, as with puns, to be filled with tension and meanings so penetrating that, in any other form, they would be difficult to accept.

If his humor is often embarrassing, his titles, like *Restricted Man*, are frustrating. The image here is a wonderfully ominous fantasy without specific or obvious reference, but the title seems to imply that we should be able to figure out not only how the man is restricted, but why. Neither, of course, is possible, or necessary.

Uelsmann's use of titles was an attempt to assist the viewer in recognizing his own interpretation of the world's inherent strangeness that he was discovering could be made overt. He was also a well-informed student of the history of photography, having studied with Beaumont Newhall at R I T, and he was familiar with the unbroken tradition of narrative titles given to works of art. Even the Dadaists and Surrealists, whose works are most closely related to Uelsmann's, used oblique literary titles. Therefore, it was natural for him to affix titles to his works in the beginning. The title was the finalization of a piece; a work seemed incomplete without it. Only within the last two or three decades has it become acceptable to artist and public alike to leave paintings or photographs untitled.

Uelsmann gave up titling his photographs for the most part by 1962. He had received considerable criticism from his peers on the matter, and his own dissatisfaction grew as he tried to find verbal equivalents for essentially visual experiences. He never began with a definite concept and then tried to illustrate it photographically. His photographs, from the very first and simplest (straight or multiple), have been the result of visual discovery. Any titles were afterthoughts, or were at least created after the completion of the photograph. Today more than ninety percent of all of the photographs he has made are untitled. Titles have not been eliminated altogether, however; from time to time, the temptation has been too great and in a moment of irresistible humor or when exactly the right words have come to mind, Uelsmann has succumbed (as in *All American Sunset, 1971*, figure 17). It is also

Figure 17. *1971 All-American Sunset*

interesting to note that he ceased titling his works at about the same time he wrote his first manifesto (1962). For Uelsmann titling was by and large another means of developing his own aesthetic in his formative period. Once he had set forth his intentions in the manifesto, his subsequent works were liberated, in effect, from the burden of titles.

In 1959, his last year at Indiana University, Uelsmann had two experiences that helped confirm the future direction of his work. Up to that point, he had been moving only tentatively in a particular direction. The first experience was seeing a combination print by Arthur Siegel; he recalls that he felt it revealed an inadequate technique, and he knew he could do better. The fact that Siegel, a leading contemporary artist, considered the technique respectable, along with Uelsmann's confidence that he could make better combination prints, pushed him into full commitment to the technique. The second experience, related to the making of one of his own photographs (figure 18), was of a different kind, and it seems (at least as he wrote about it in retrospect) to have had a significant impact on the way he perceived an artist's obligation to the integrity of his medium and its presumed boundaries:

*I once came upon a Civil War tombstone in a small cemetery. The light was dramatically breaking across the plain. I was very moved. I made one photograph and then for reasons which I honestly cannot personally explain, I picked up a tiny flower and in my own private ritual wedged it next to the soldier's gun. That was important to me in that it was the first time that I had in any way imposed myself upon the subject matter.*[10]

By 1963, Uelsmann's multiple-printing technique was sufficiently perfected for him to take it for granted. As a result, the imagery of his photographs exploded into an apparently unlimited array of surprising combinations of forms and subjects. The psychological element of the imagery developed more slowly, however, and did not reach maturity until the late sixties.

During his last year at Indiana University, Uelsmann enrolled in a course in American folklore, and after his move to the South in 1960 to join the University of Florida faculty, he became, in his own words, "a collector with a camera." This was his first trip to the South; thus it was a new environment for him. The entire countryside was fresh with

Figure 18. *1959 Monument to War*

dramatic folk art, like the gravestone in the Civil War cemetery, and with unbelievably exotic flora and fauna. The social structure was also new to him, with customs of far greater force than those of the society he had left behind in the Midwest.

His photographs from the early sixties are carefully constructed images drawn from a mixture of subjects, both highly symbolic and formal. In recent lectures he has spoken of symmetry and spatial manipulation as the two major aesthetic concerns developed in his work during this period. These interests, combined with a mastery of multiple-image technique, allowed a new motif to emerge from his intuitive way of working. He began creating visual metaphors, but his use of metaphor was different from that of Minor White. White's use of visual metaphor was so subtle that it was not apparent until the viewer had gained an understanding of his aesthetic stance and the meaning of his titles, and experience in his rhetorical vocabulary. Uelsmann, on the other hand, sought a much more straightforward use of visual metaphor. His images were intended to express, as indeed they do, the vocabulary of an unanticipated nonverbal world, but in an obviously metaphorical way. Freed from reality by a willingness to delve into a fantasy world of subjects, he took as his first aesthetic tools symmetry and space. Referring to a photograph of a seedpod made at this time, Uelsmann said:

*The thing that was most appealing to me was the fluctuating space, the duality of the space, the way in which the image could be read at two different levels — that was the exciting thing. This challenged the whole concept of the neatly resolved metamorphose-type image. It freed me in simple terms. From then on, I began to work with some ideas, exploring this near-far kind of spatial relationship. Symmetry, it seems to me, is something that has been thought of*

Figure 19. *1965*

*as relatively dull until recently. The Now generation, with its psychedelic art concerns, has shown us that once again symmetry can be quite exciting. And in photography, certainly symmetry is the unanticipated; it is the unexpected image.*[11]

Uelsmann's conscious exploration of symmetrical forms and a "near-far" space relationship is generally evident as the dominant element in his photographs of the 1960s. Figures 19 and 20 illustrate the methods he primarily employed and, to some extent, continues to employ in order to integrate these structural concepts into visual metaphor. In figure 19, a large object looms in the foreground, dividing the picture area into two equal vertical zones, while the background recedes to a ground line that further divides the frame into two horizontal parts. The extreme close-up and large scale of the foreground object is a compositional device used by many artists other than Uelsmann, most notably, of course, Ansel Adams and Edward Weston. But the device performs different compositional and structural functions in the work of each artist who has used it. In Uelsmann's photographs, the object is generally esoteric, or alien to the environmental context. This immediately establishes the image as metaphoric or surreal for the viewer. In figure 19, the object's scale and placement in the foreground were probably the result of random experiment despite the fact that the image is a consistent compositional device in his work:

*I collect fragments that I respond to. They might later become part of something I would call a meaningful image. A simple thing like a piece of paper blowing in the wind might serve as the foreground of an image yet to be realized. Rarely do I decide while I'm taking the photograph where the element will end up. Sometimes it's obvious that a particular old home might serve as a background or a particular rock might work in the foreground. But most of the time I've no real knowledge of where it's going to end up.*[12]

In many of his photographs with vertical symmetry (for example, figure 20), mirror-like images are used to create symmetrical duplication. The mechanical device of flopping the negative or using two identical negatives, one flopped, is intentionally left obvious to the viewer. It offers the peculiar kind of visual pleasure inherent to symmetry. The open use of the device recalls Uelsmann's statement that he is fond of strawberries because "they don't hide their seeds." These mirror images often join the subjects to create an altogether new form that heightens the sense of enigma. In figure 20, the two nudes become buttresslike figures supporting a more fluid form that dominates the center of the photograph. Obviously, the central form is an organic visual metaphor for the reproductive anatomy of woman, repeating its theme in multiple layers of transparency (space) and convolution.

When Uelsmann says that symmetry is unexpected in photography, he is implying that it is not perceived in landscapes or conglomerate subjects; hence, symmetry is foreign to straight documentary photography. Since his own photographs developed from documentary interests, the use of symmetry — which was thus an imposition on an image — and manipulation became synonymous to him.

Symmetry in Uelsmann's compositions is more than a creative device. It also reflects a dialectical philosophy or approach to art and life in which reality and fantasy result in a synthesis greater than the parts. This synthesis, Uelsmann believes, is revelatory of his innermost being. It is the "self" that characterizes the subjectivity of twentieth-century art. The aesthetic of self is a motif that embraces concepts like "expressionism" and "equivalence" (the latter meaning an equation of self with emotional experience and with cognition of life), and the various technical and ideological "isms" in art since the turn of the century as well. This concept of self as manifested by twentieth-century artists, including Uelsmann, is not a guise for ego, which would simply be an act of seeing all of life in a mirror. Rather, it is a compulsion to project onto reality the illusive, translucent meaning of creative human forces in the context of a coldly physical world.

Peter Bunnell's first essay on Uelsmann referred to the latter's sense of self by describing his humorous exterior, "his speech, his mildly eccentric clothes, his mania for collecting bric-a-brac," and his "consummate endurance on the grand pianola." All of this, Bunnell suggested, "concealed an intensity of concern for life and personal doubt" about life's meaning.[13] It was this essay by Bunnell in *Aperture* in 1970 (along with Uelsmann's exhibition at the Museum of Modern Art in 1967) that launched his photography into the mainstream of critical attention. Despite the growing acclaim his work was beginning to receive and the resultant spread of his influence, it was (as it remains) inimitable.

28

Figure 20. *1965*

The few attempts at imitation that have surfaced have been extremely inadequate and superficial, dependent upon copying his technique alone. While the same could be said of the mass imitation of the works of photographers like Lee Friedlander and Garry Winogrand, the techniques of these artists are more susceptible to well-crafted imitation than is Uelsmann's. Imitation of techniques and styles, however, no matter how pervasive, is meaningless. It is the spread of ideas that creates movements and provides the linkage we call influence. In this sense, Uelsmann's published discussions of his technique and his aesthetics have expanded our appreciation of the medium by changing our ideas about what a photograph is. His discussions suggest that "photography" can be considered as an umbrella for all kinds of photographic techniques and ideas, not just a narrowly defined medium.

Uelsmann has had an impact on the field similar to that of Robert Heinecken. This is not to suggest that their ideologies or aesthetic interests are in any way alike. But both have accepted, for their own work, ideas and concepts outside the general traditions of the medium, and both have made use of unique, nontraditional techniques. Both have been more interested in dissecting reality than in reflecting it. Heinecken's early works give evidence of his studies in printmaking and painting, but it is evidence of the media themselves, rather than of the ideas of those who taught them, while Uelsmann's reveal the thinking of his mentors to a greater degree. Henry Holmes Smith, in his own work and in his teaching, espoused both subjectivity and a healthy respect for classical literary ideals. Both attitudes are characteristic of Uelsmann's early work and, in fact, can be found periodically throughout his career. References to antiquity recur especially. In a letter to Smith in 1960, Uelsmann acknowledged the intensity of the debt he felt:

*For now let me say that near the end of my Indiana stay I became increasingly conscious of the extent to which my images were "right" and "true" to me, as opposed to being theatrical and technical feats performed in areas of secondary interest. Now that I have some understanding of those areas which belong to my world, I hope that I will be able to proceed in depth. I am deeply indebted to you, Henry, for a great deal more than a photographic education.*[14]

Influence, if handled with maturity and self-confidence, is like a good plant food, which accelerates growth and strengthens a healthy plant, increasing the quality of its fruit. But no amount of nutrient can benefit a weak plant, and, given in excess, it will make that plant fruitless or destroy it. Uelsmann, from the beginning of his career, had the ability to master the influences that touched his life and work. Intuitively, he knew the degree to which one must listen before speaking, and the subtle difference between absorbing and merely borrowing.

The aesthetic elements that make up Uelsmann's work are far more numerous and complex in detail than can possibly be explored exhaustively here. This difficulty is reinforced by the fact that he has produced an average of one hundred prints per year for twenty-five years. There are, however, dominant motifs and themes in his early work that indicate the character of his aesthetic predilections. Such motifs increase in number as his career progresses but, for the first half of the 1960s, those of greatest interest are: images reflecting his concern with "self"; the floating object, introduced and used repeatedly in these years; and images developing the theme of "the predicament of Man."

Figure 21.
*1965 Self-Portrait as an Incurable Romantic*

Uelsmann's exploration of his own person as the subject of his works is represented most clearly by his self-portraits. These photographs are seldom simple mirror images, and, although they first appeared in the 1960s, Uelsmann continues the exploration by making self-portraits today.

*I occasionally do self-portraits. It seems to me that many times we forget about the threatening qualities that the camera has; we readily point it at people and they respond to it. I think it's a very healthy thing that on occasion photographers should get around in front of the camera. I must admit that I also see this as a very personal theatre, a sort of theatre of the self, a very private performance which you are essentially "doing for yourself."* [15]

When Uelsmann photographs himself or, more correctly, makes a photograph of himself, he is more concerned with making a study of the interior of the man than with making a

Figure 22. *1964*

physiographic representation. Although he is recognizable in such works as *Self-Portrait as an Incurable Romantic* (figure 21), the representational factor is less important than the role he has given himself to play in the photograph. In fact, more recent self-portraits are even less dependent on his physical image. For example, in *Small Woods Where I Met Myself, 1967* (plate 48), Uelsmann's image is not present at all, yet the title of the work makes it clear that the concern is with self.

Uelsmann is preoccupied with his spiritual state and the level of cognizance he can convey to the viewer concerning its meaning. He claims to believe in angels, but one does not know whether this belief is based in iconic fascination or serious metaphysics. In any case, he has included angels in his self-portraits, as in figure 21, and in a work from 1973 entitled *Agony of Flight* (figure 28). In the latter, he has given himself wings, to become the ecstasy of flight itself. In an even more recent self-portrait, entitled *Animus/Anima, 1978* (plate 107), he has gone to the heart of the matter and attempted to visualize soul and purpose without the trappings of angels. This use of angels is, of course, an oblique yet literal way of expressing his concern for self, treating the theme with either great light-heartedness or deep passion.

The floating or levitating object that is so common to Uelsmann's entire body of work was first introduced into his photographs about 1964. Prior to that time, there were a few works in which objects did not actually float, but shared the two-dimensional space of the picture with a naturalistic representation (for example, figure 31, plate 30). But in 1964 the objects began to levitate in an illusionistic environment of convincing three-dimensional space. In addition, as in figure 22, the floating object began to assume a character seemingly inappropriate to its environment and became mysterious and enigmatic. These qualitites have remained constants of the floating object in Uelsmann's later work. To the viewer, the puzzle does not lie in the levitation so much as in why that object is in that environment. With this pictorial device, Uelsmann makes the inappropriate appear appropriate and the unbelievable believable. He also opened up almost unlimited possibilities for nonliteral — visual — representation and exploration of his aesthetic interests. His two avenues of search for *anima*, through studies of self and through fanciful defiance of earthly reality, were now leading to the same place.

As his work has matured and expanded in concept, the number of avenues explored has increased, as have the points to which they lead. The predominant theme explored by Uelsmann from the early 1960s to the present day is what he has called "the predicament of Man":

*I am very much concerned with the way man is prevented from being certain things by conditions that exist outside of himself. Frequently, these are conditions over which he has no control, yet their effect is immediate and real. Man prevented by economic conditions, by social tradition, by education, by his physical being. . . .* [16]

Uelsmann made another photograph entitled *Restricted Man* (figure 23) in 1961, the year before he wrote about "the predicament of Man" in his manifesto. While this photograph represents a less subtle approach to the theme he described, it nevertheless embodies the essential characteristics of his concern. With his development as an artist, his exploration of man against the world shifted to man against the universe, and the man himself (or woman in some cases) became less boxed in by the conditions of his situation. The hardships to be endured, however, became increasingly more ominous and alienating. As Uelsmann's self-confidence about violating the traditional rules of photography grew, so did the freedom with which he allowed random elements of his conscious predilections to come together. The result was more sophisticated "predicaments," of more outrageous portent: humans and nature in metamorphosis; impending physical dangers; and strange, psychologically probing environments.

While the predicament-of-Man theme was a major force in Uelsmann's photographs of the 1960s and has remained a recurring one since, it is today only one of many philosophical directions in his work. The seeds of the visual manifestations of his philosophy were planted when Uelsmann set down what he called "Random Thoughts on Photography." This document, his first manifesto, is published here in its entirety for the first time.

Figure 23. *1961 Restricted Man*

# Random Thoughts on Photography

*January 1962*

*The following represents a random sampling of thoughts on photography. No effort has been made to develop a concise philosophical system or to proceed logically to a profound conclusion. If many of my statements are ambiguous or contradictory, that is as it should be, for I am young and my thoughts are in constant and necessary flux. I cannot guarantee that I will find the thoughts that I am having today acceptable or relevant by the end of the week. I have above all else tried to be honest and true to myself.*

*The commitment on the part of the photographer cannot involve compromise. Photography for the artist can and should be a vigorous and vital event. I personally believe in a degree of involvement with life that transcends the "rational." (When you laugh it should be loud and long and when you feel sad you should weep!) I do not mean to imply that this involvement is irrational; perhaps non-rational is the best term. It seems to me that a multitude of daily human "events" occur outside of an intellectualized rationale. These are intense, albeit nebulous, events in which the human elements are such that the propensity for an honest insight is greatly increased. There have been moments when I have attempted to "remove" myself in order to study and comment on this thing we call human existence. It never works for me. The images that result from this attitude are rarely more than cliché. Although many things have caused me to reflect and reconsider, I am, and I suppose will always be, basically a humanist. Whenever I attempt to back up in order to get a greater perspective, I fall all over people; they push me; tickle me; talk back to me; curse me and cajole me, all the while forcing me back into complete and immediate involvement. So it is that I will never assume the role of the prophet.*

*My images deal with what I understand to be the* real *world, the here and now. These images grow out of problems, emotions, and ideas. They are almost never motivated by subject matter. I have nothing against subject matter; it's just that it has never been a primary consideration. It occurs only as a by-product of the visual statement. Sometimes I feel that I* am on the first page of a personal visual dictionary that I am slowly evolving in an effort to define my own existence. Physically I am committed to life (ideologically too) and I am attempting to come to grips with it on a human level. I have no particular plan of attack other than I get out of bed every morning. The adventure of the particular moment excites me the most.

I have never overtly attempted to formulate a mode of behavior. This, if it has occurred, has come about naturally (and intuitively). Unconsciously one slowly creates elaborate patterns of expectancy for all of the things that belong to one's immediate world. The effect of this behavior is to clarify life so that it doesn't appear to be the series of unrelated erratic events that it really is. We condition ourselves so that life occurs with routine normalcy. In my personal investigation of life, the atypical event has been both a prod and a chief source of insight for me, in that the immediate by-product of such an event is a reconsideration of the accepted norm. It is a very direct way of attacking complacency. An interesting problem is that the atypical event, by its very nature, does not lend itself to planning. It is difficult to force such an event. I have in no way aspired to become a mystic; I abhor the notion. However, I must confess that atypical events have occurred in my life with uncanny regularity and I now believe that some long forgotten ancient god has singled me out as his worldly toy.

These deviations from our own patterns of expectancy have functioned as cracks in the facade which prevents us from contact with the essence of our existence. I used to worry about developing an approach to life and photography. This is no longer a consideration. An approach, if there is such a thing, evolves out of a commitment to life and is not to be sought after as a separate entity. At one point, when I first began to work with the "multiple image," I attempted to codify two separate images into a third which would function as a unique separate image, the whole being something greater than the independent parts. I feel that many of my multiple images work this way; however, I no longer consider this a valid criterion for evaluation of such images. The unresolved multiple image has its own kind of content, equally valid.

I am not the darkroom "nut" that many may assume. All aspects of the photographic process are open for exploration and re-evaluation. I merely attempt to approach each stage of the process with an adventuresome spirit. On occasion I have attempted to backtrack in an *effort to determine the means by which a specific, personally meaningful, image was created. I have never been successful. In some instances, the negatives involved in a multiple print were taken six months apart. What strange circumstances brought them to the surface of my consistently chaotic desk on a day I felt like printing remains a mystery. My images emerge out of a form of human encounter and not a technical one.*

*I am involved with a kind of reality that transcends surface reality. More than physical reality, it is emotional, irrational, intellectual, and psychological. It is because of the fact that these other forms of reality don't exist as specific, tangible objects that I can honestly say that subject matter is only a minor consideration which proceeds after the fact and not before. (We don't select a handsome group of words and then try to say something; but rather we begin speaking and the words come out as the result of our efforts to say something meaningful.) Too many people tend to define the creative act in photography solely in terms of the selection of appropriate subject matter. To a certain extent it may be so, but it can also be much more than this. All too frequently the motives that go into the selection of subject matter have little or nothing to do with the probable content of the resulting images. To photograph a person because you like their complexion is an entirely different motive than photographing someone because you love them. Perhaps the most crucial problem in serious photography today is the acceptance of irrelevant secondary motives as though they were intense, relevant, primary ones. I do not mean to imply that my own motives have always been of the highest order. When I first became involved with serious photography, my motives were frequently irrelevant and superficial; I thought almost exclusively in terms of subject matter. Within the past few years, my attitudes and motives have begun to expand and grow. This transition has been a relatively natural one, although a constant effort was made to bring it about. I wasn't always aware of what I was seeking, but purely pictorial motives made me restless.*

*A large body of my imagery may fall under the general title of "The predicament of Man." I am very much concerned with the way man is prevented from being certain things by conditions that exist outside of himself. Frequently, these are conditions over which he has no control, yet their effect is immediate and real. Man prevented by economic conditions, by social tradition, by education, by his physical being. . . . I am attempting to create an intensive awareness of the existence of these restrictions. I am particularly concerned about whether or not they have a reasonable ethical foundation; although I feel such an investigation will logically follow.*

*The span of a photographic aesthetic which I can now endorse is almost without end (from the pantheistic hymns to nature made by Adams to the totemic constructions which grow out of the intellect of Sommer). The act of image making may run the range from a prima donna technical performance (frequently done to assure the philistines that craftsmanship is still alive) to one in which the human event is so overpowering that the photographic gesture is as unconscious as a soft stomach rumble.*

*My images are personal but I sincerely hope that they have significant implications for others; although this is not a consideration when I am involved in the photographic act. My attitude toward the audience is impassive; although I must confess a slight fear of becoming widely accepted.*

*My feelings about the future of serious photography range from one of anxious optimism to one of sincere doubt. Serious photography is still very much a mystery for me. I have many intense emotions about the subject that are in apparent opposition. It is both easy and difficult; at times it is impossible. It may be fun; it is work; frequently it is painful. It is so intimate, yet public.*

*Personally, I am committed to the medium and I make no apologies for it. I have gradually confused photography with life and, as the result of this, I believe that I am able to work out of myself at an almost pre-cognitive level. You must realize that my photographic existence is in a genesis state. The images which I have made this past year excite me a great deal more than the ones I made a year ago, and almost any of the photographs that I made before that time I can pass off as tentative groping gestures with no real significance other than perhaps a personally historical one. I am unable to pinpoint the exact conditions which enabled me to come to grips with certain aspects of my own life. I am too close and involved with the event to be retrospective about it.*

# 1967-1975

TODAY . . . NOW . . . GOD ONLY KNOWS. *I keep imagining that I find notes on my desk like "Stieglitz phoned while you were out." If I could only have been there when he called; perhaps he would know what I'm up to. I range from paralyzing self-pity to incredible productivity. I have long been nourished by enigma. I'm not trying to solve anything. My priorities are shifting. My questions have a better "feel" to them and I'm still learning about being Alive.*

*Believe me, there is always doubt about what you are doing. It has never interfered much with my productivity but it's always there, filling the air with questions. It took me a long time to realize that constant sustained questioning is capable of contributing to a healthy state. Offhand I would say two conditions must exist: first, the process (camera or darkroom) must be trusted to have equal responsibility in forming the questions, and second, one must establish some sense of connoisseurship that helps the questioning process grow in terms of precision and intensity.*

The above is from a letter written by Uelsmann to Peter Bunnell in February 1974, a year before publication of *Silver Meditations*, which marks the end of the period discussed in this section. During these eight years Uelsmann received his greatest exposure through exhibition, publication, and honors. His style was now distinct and recognizable. His execution and craftsmanship in photomontage were flawless, and critics began to talk about his work on the basis of his aesthetics, no longer dwelling on his technique.

The year 1967 was an almost magical turning point. John Szarkowski organized a one-person exhibition of his photographs at the Museum of Modern Art; he received a Guggenheim Fellowship; *Camera* magazine in Switzerland featured his photographs; and significant American publications like *Aperture* and *Contemporary Photographer* included major coverage of his work and ideas.

Uelsmann's aesthetic premise for his unique, psychologically draped imagery is stated conclusively in the letter to Bunnell quoted above. Had his remarks been public, they would have put to rest the critical misstatement that his photographs were surrealistic. As a body, his photographs defy any single categorization, just as each of his photographs defies literal interpretation. What appears surreal in his work is most often the product of an absurd or unbelievable juxtaposition of objects or situations. Such has been the case from the very first successful "surreal" image of his student days. However, the stream-of-consciousness method of the founders of Surrealism is rarely employed by Uelsmann. In fact, Uelsmann's *selection* of subjects for juxtaposition contradicts the Surrealist dictum of automatism.

*Experimentation involves inventing a language at the same time you're using it. I make proof sheets of everything. The negatives are kept in numerical order, but I let proof sheets get mixed up. I have found that I can pick up a hundred proof sheets and, in a matter of five minutes, find the particular image I want to work with. I need a retrievable system that is not complex, one that includes a very loose structure for proof sheets. They are my visual dictionary and/or diary. They represent everything that I've seen and responded to over a period of many years. . . .*

*Because of the way I work, a lot of my proof sheets involve the collecting of things visually. Rarely do I decide while I'm taking the photograph where the element will end up. . . .*

*When I get ready to print, I sit down with a stack of proof sheets. Usually the things that are most recent are on top, but they get rapidly mixed with the others. I look at these proof sheets and try to find clues to things that might work together. Sometimes (and this is a mental state) I'll sit down and, in half an hour, I can make more little notes of things I want to try than I could possibly do in a week.*[17]

Figure 24. *1970*

Uelsmann makes the absurd appear believable and the incongruous convincing (figure 24)—which Surrealism rarely intends or achieves—by a method he has called "in-process discovery," a term he absorbed from colleagues in the painting department of the University of Florida. However, for Uelsmann, in-process discovery is more than a harmonious relationship between medium and cognition. It is in essence a gestalt position, in which creativity is viewed in terms of one's ability to associate dissimilar elements in meaningful ways and to restructure the entire stimulus field.[18] To disassociate known subject relationships (reality) and reassociate them in new but perhaps mysterious ways is the aesthetic thread that runs throughout his work. When Uelsmann speaks of "questions" in referring to his work, he is promoting "doubt" as a positive and essential force within in-process discovery. Time and again he refers to this point, as in the quotations that open this section and in the following:

*It is important that we maintain a continual open dialogue with our materials and process; that we are constantly questioning and in turn being questioned. In terms of my own develop-ment, I have found the recognition of questions more provocative than the provision of an-swers. Often, confident that we have the right answers, we fail to ask enough questions, and then our seeming confidence fogs our vision and the inconceivable remains truly uncon-ceived.*[19]

While several substantial essays were written about Uelsmann during the period from 1967 to 1975, the most insightful were those by William E. Parker and Peter Bunnell. Both wrote basic critical essays on Uelsmann's photographs for *Aperture*. Parker's article of 1967, entitled "Uelsmann's Unitary Reality," was unquestionably the more esoteric, and probed the psychohistory of Uelsmann's imagery with authority and poetry, in a machine-gun fire of prose. Parker saw Uelsmann's imagery as wholly symbolic and based on psychological archetypes. Image after image was dissected in an attempt to throw light on what others had perceived as hidden and surreal. Within the limits of what one can understand of the psychologizing content and of one's belief in its fundamentalist approach, the essay is brilliant. But Parker's article was not widely read, and, although it was the first substantial treatment of Uelsmann's work, it did not have much effect upon the field in terms of broadening the understanding of his photography. In spite of this, the essay did serve to promote Uelsmann's emergence into the arena of popular awareness and crit-ical inquiry. A certain measure of credibility was gained, of course, through *Aperture*'s reputation as a leading publication of fine photography and the stature of the journal's edi-tor, Minor White.

Three years later, Peter Bunnell published his essay in *Aperture*; although not as comprehensive a treatment as Parker's, it offered a clearer understanding of Uelsmann as an artist and a foundation for approaching his work in traditional aesthetic terms. But it was Bunnell's essay in *Silver Meditations*, the first major monograph on Uelsmann in book form, that, through its extraordinary flow of language and ideas, gave the photography community its first real glimpse of the meaning behind Uelsmann's unique style and solitary aesthetic approach. Published in 1975, it found Uelsmann at a high point in his career in terms of critical attention. The book was perfectly timed, and it sold over 15,000 copies.[20] Uelsmann and Bunnell had been close friends since the late fifties, so his understanding of the work is not surprising. The following passage from the *Silver Meditations* essay sums up the direction of Uelsmann's work around 1975:

*In contrast to his earlier pictures, Uelsmann's work in recent years has become less graphically dominating in terms of what may be seen as the relatively simple and harmonious counterpoint of objects and forms. Since 1972 the picture space in his images has been filled in a more total and stressing fashion reflecting his own more complex psychic nature. He has reached the point where the work has turned in upon itself, where the master of craft has moved outside of illusions and conscious showmanship to a more introspective state of affairs where one can no longer tell so easily what is going on.*

Indeed, Uelsmann's photographs of this time became more complex in their range of meanings and were more subtle in the use of traditional devices (disparity of scale, exaggerated perspective, and so on) found in his photographs before 1967. His imagery was now more obviously introspective and concentrated in his favorite areas of mystery, fantasy, and absurdity. Especially characteristic of the change in his work during this period was the use of humor; Bunnell noted that the recent work would be "much less apt to amuse the viewer."[21] This is not to suggest that Uelsmann's particular brand of humor was no longer present in his work. It had simply become more subtle, although still dependent on parody (figure 25). Henry Holmes Smith had first commented on Uelsmann's use of humor as early as 1964 in an essay he had written for the quarterly *Contemporary Photographer*:

*The comic is able to pay attention and therefore can make unexpected connections between otherwise unconnected fragments known to all of us.*

*In his present work Uelsmann is using the skill of the comic to make some of these connections,*

Figure 25. *1973*

*but he is not concerned with any important comic effect. What in his daily life has been re-fracted, he restores in a strange way we all can recognize. What may have been a joke or a hurt turned into a joke takes a different turn in the photographs. The funny becomes gro-tesque, a grotesquery capable at times of arousing the feeling of horror. . . .*

*I hope I will not be misunderstood when I suggest that here we may see the vaudeville per-former's Hamlet (the comic playing a tragic role). Some of the awkwardness, and all of the striving for dramatic intensity, are present. Yet in many of the pictures there is an undeniable sense of reality felt and expressed.*[22]

44

It has never been easy, and remains difficult (even for Uelsmann), to tell exactly what is going on in his images, except in his overtly humorous works and in his portraits. These last two groups have generally been straightforward, without allegory, myth, or mystery (figure 26).

Uelsmann's photographs made between 1967 and 1975 were interpreted by various authors largely on the basis of personal biases (for example, William Parker's use of Jungian archetypes), but it is also important to note that the works inspired such interpretation because their symbolism was less obvious. Uelsmann, as has been noted, often directed the symbolism of his earlier work through titles (for example, *Apocalypse II, 1967*, figure 27), but after 1967, he rarely used titles and, when he did, they were usually less meaningful. Although some symbolic element remains in even his most recent work, symbolism is no longer pervasive. As quoted earlier, Uelsmann acknowledged his use of symbols, but with qualifications: "I think of my photographs as being obviously symbolic, but not symbolically obvious."[23] His twisting of words is as playful as his mixture of humor and symbol. The artist in Uelsmann is like the Dalai Lama, a giggling mystic with a very serious and complex intent.

Figure 26. *1973 Ansel*

At the turn of the century pictorialists used a cloak of Greek and Roman classicism in order to make eroticism acceptable. Similarly, Uelsmann disguises his content by making the symbol progressively less abstract; the often romantic nature of his subjects cloaks their intellectual and emotional provocativeness, and their disposition lends a pictorial quality to Uelsmann's work. The eroticism of his photographs containing nudes (predominantly female) is derived from sensuous poses and attitudes that nevertheless are without overt sexual implications. It is an erotic romanticism, and in this Uelsmann's work differs greatly from that of numerous contemporary photographers who purge their work of all forms of romanticism in response to current social attitudes and mores that assume that any form of idealism is a subliminal attempt to hide the truth. What they lose in this process is an understanding of the value of emotional content as a prime purveyor of aesthetic energy. Uelsmann has remained undaunted by a trend that has promoted banal and purely decorative subjects, and he continues to include emotion in his aesthetic:

*By our cameras we are introduced to an endless array of trees, clouds, rocks, people, feelings, experiences, and so on. We wander through this varied landscape as contemporary archeologists, poets, and explorers essentially searching in our own internally directed way. Each click of the shutter becomes an emotional investment, and a part of the world becomes our visual possession.*[24]

With Uelsmann's statement likening us to contemporary archeologists, poets, and explorers in an internally directed search for meaning in our environment, the simple symbol in his work begins to give way to a more adventurous and complicated motif — myth-making. We generally think of myths as stories from antiquity, most often telling of the pleasures and pains of man arising from the challenges of his gods. To the extent that mental images, before words, gave birth to such mythology, there is a correlation with Uelsmann's imagery. Certainly there is also a correlation between the theme of predicament in classical mythology and the "predicament of Man" that preoccupies Uelsmann. His myth-making is of a more spontaneous nature, however, not requiring or implying reference to the laws of nature, culture, or deities. Nor do his myths, as visual entities, illustrate morals, mores, or lessons. He creates parasymbolic stories that represent the in-

Figure 27. *1967 Apocalypse II*

tangible, nonverbal nature of our mental visions and emotions. What is drawn from our psychic sources exists with difficulty elsewhere, but for Uelsmann, as for the ancient Greeks, myth can represent what cannot really exist.[25]

The frequent repetition of his subjects' plight or environment make one less satisfied that aleatory forces or dream consciousness play as significant a role in his work as they do in traditional mythology. Describing the difference between myth and dream, Joseph Campbell, in *The Hero with a Thousand Faces*, provides an interpretation of myth that offers a possible foundation for the kind found in Uelsmann's photographs:

*Dream is the personalized myth, myth the depersonalized dream; both myth and dream are symbolic in the same general way of the dynamics of the psyche. But in the dream the forms are quirked by the peculiar troubles of the dreamer, whereas in myth the problems and solutions shown are directly valid for all mankind.*[26]

47

In making his photographs Uelsmann is careful not to invoke the purely personal vernacular of Surrealism or to accept its proselytization of the dogma of the unconscious. He purposely speaks of his confidence in his ability to work in a "preconscious" manner. In the use of this term he reveals that in making photographs he gives equal consideration to his aesthetic predilections and to his intuitive response to subjects, objects, and environmental situations. Through his final choice and combinations of subjects he creates associative forms that appear unreal, yet are convincing and harmonious in superrealistic terms. These photo-images are the product of a visual vernacular that has been cultivated from the unrestricted provinces of the mind; the mind, rather than the known world—the expected source for photography—is the referent. It is because Uelsmann's photographs are so convincing that a pinpoint interpretation at first seems necessary in order to justify our belief in them and consequently our acceptance of them. However, if Uelsmann's photographs are to be "understood," one must look at them with the same eye that has learned over the centuries to accept and embrace all possibilities in the aesthetic realm. Among the factors playing a role in viewers' contact with art works through the ages have been individual empathy, emotional stimulation, intellectual challenge, and—the irrefutable requirement—visual pleasure. It is the pervasive "witness to nature" concept of photography that misleads the viewer into expecting Uelsmann's imagery to have rational links to the world and to psychological explanations for human actions and conditions as revealed by science and medicine. Uelsmann's photographs are planned, composed, structured, and intentionally pushed to the edge of reason for the sake not only of questioning what photography can be, but of testing the boundaries of cognitive perception itself (figure 28).

This domain of visual mythology evolved out of Uelsmann's use of symbols. Such a mythology is entirely visual and does not relate in form to any known narrative sources, either historical ones or the myths of primitive cultures.

Uelsmann's myth-making is not generalized in the body of his work. Each myth is individual to each photograph and is complete in itself. Each represents a kind of story telling about Uelsmann's personal journey between visual discovery and visual creation. Within the sphere of these myths, emotions are set free, humor and seriousness are often

Figure 28. *1973 Agony of Flight*

inseparable, and enigma is the godhead of his chosen associative forms. In Uelsmann's words: "If one accepts the fact that you can impose yourself on subject matter, then perhaps you can literally create subject matter."[27]

The scenario for each myth in Uelsmann's photographs lacks a beginning and an end, unlike written myths or those of oral tradition. Rather, these visual mythologies contain disparate elements of unlived, but psychically recognizable, experiences.

Uelsmann's faith in in-process discovery and his evolution from simple symbol to myth invokes the spirit of a Latin phrase painted by Giorgio de Chirico on his self-portrait of 1911 *Et quid amabo nisi quod aenigma est?* (And what shall I love, if not the enigma?) It is more than a coincidence that in an early (undated) set of notes he made for addressing students on aesthetic motivation, Uelsmann wrote:

*I've been wondering lately about how many ways one can give one's self to photography (and life) and still be effective. Where is that proper balance that will allow for meaningful involvement in the many tasks that life is presenting me at this time? I've been an "image maker" my entire life and I know I must continue to create my visual myth. Right now my personal search is more exciting than ever before. The possibilities seem infinite and I'm eager to return to my darkroom, for I know discovery awaits.*

The mythological subject divisions in Uelsmann's photographs, created by virtue of repeated situations and subject attitudes, allow the possibility of traditional archetypes as seen by William Parker. Among these are cosmogony, hero, earth woman, mother goddess, flood, death, apocalypse, paradise, and morphology. Such archetypes *do* exist, but their discovery requires that the viewer have a desire to discover them within the individual works.

To view Uelsmann's photography of the late sixties and early seventies in terms of photo–myth-making relieves the critic of the timeworn, even worn out, amateur psychologizing first introduced by the Surrealists and perpetuated by the critics of avant-garde painting of the 1950s; "amateur" because few historians, critics, or viewers are trained or qualified to write about, or to interpret, art in such terms. In addition, the use of a vocabulary modishly adopted from the vernacular of psychology has not, in fact, contributed to a better understanding of Uelsmann's photographs. Rather, the result has been more like name-dropping—for example, "Surrealism." An exception to such usage is, of course, Parker's. His thesis is less didactic, and furthermore, he is more qualified in his knowledge of psychology than most others.

The critical literature on Uelsmann, beginning in 1967, is as often by him as it is about him. A particularly interesting example is a 1967 issue of *Contemporary Photographer* that includes essays by Uelsmann's teacher-mentor Ralph Hattersley, Uelsmann himself, and Robert Heinecken, who shares in some degree a philosophy of the medium with

Uelsmann.[28] A few random quotations from Hattersley's essay, entitled "Give Your Creative Mind a Chance," will provide flavor and suggest the direction embodied in the title:

*Every child still is, until adults — and other children — force him to drive his creative mind into hiding, where it now becomes what is called the subconscious or unconscious. . . .*

*Memory systems drive the true child-self even deeper into hiding, where everything is remembered but from whence hardly anything can be recalled. . . .*

*In terms of the child-self, creative-self, there is no such thing as a good habit.*

How Hattersley's thinking and attitudes affected Uelsmann becomes clear in reading this essay. Uelsmann has attempted to remain childlike through his humor and through his willingness to stay innocent of the fashions of contemporary photography over the years. He has faith in the value of working from the innermost reaches of his mind rather than in taking a more calculated approach to his work. If one looks for outside influences on Uelsmann, then certainly Hattersley was one.

Uelsmann's essay in the same issue of the quarterly was really a new manifesto. Entitled "Post-Visualization," it was essentially a takeoff on Edward Weston's "pre-visualization." In the manifesto, which has become Uelsmann's best-known essay, and consequently his accepted aesthetic statement, he proposes an alternative approach to what he terms "prescribed darkroom ritual." To that ritual and the approach to photography associated with it, he also consigns "documentary" and "decisive-moment" aesthetics. Again, a few quotations provide a sense of the essay's content:

*The contemporary artist . . . is not bound to a fully conceived, pre-visioned end. His mind is kept alert to in-process discovery and a working rapport is established between the artist and his creation.*

*While it may be true, as Nathan Lyons has stated, that "the eye and the camera see more than the mind knows," is it not also conceivable that the mind knows more than the eye and the camera see?*

*By post-visualization, I refer to the willingness on the part of the photographer to revisualize the final image at any point in the entire photographic process.*

Uelsmann's post-visualization essay-manifesto was his mature evaluation of the importance of freedom and emotion imbued in him by his three teachers, Smith, Hattersley, and White. It represents the moment at which Uelsmann became secure in the aesthetics of his own photography and felt the need to share his way, as the ways of others had been shared with him. This article, more than any other at that time, identified Uelsmann as unique to the field, and the demand to publish excerpts from it has continued during the fifteen years since it first appeared.

The essay by Heinecken in the same issue of *Contemporary Photographer*, entitled "Manipulative Photography," reinforced the need to be free from pre-visualization, the same theme treated in the essays of Hattersley and Uelsmann, each artist handling it in his own way. Although it is not likely that Carl Chiarenza, the quarterly's editor, intended to put forth a position paper that would advocate a change in direction for contemporary photography, these three essays published in concert may have seemed to be just that. The strong effect of their simultaneous publication at this moment in Uelsmann's career drew unusual attention to his work. A passage from Heinecken's essay is pertinent in this connection:

*We constantly tend to misuse or misunderstand the term "reality" in reference to photographs. The photograph itself is the only thing that is real, that exists. Obviously no picture, photographic or otherwise, can hope to come close in duplicating or even simulating reality. Unless, of course, one is concerned with making photographs of things rather than photographs about things. I find the differentiation between of and about a useful one. Many pictures turn out to be limp translations of the known world instead of vital objects which create an intrinsic world of their own. (There is a vast difference between taking a picture and making a photograph.)*

The wide range of exposure and critical attention in photography magazines, catalogues, and major exhibitions greatly contributed to the meteoric rise of Uelsmann's reputation during the late 1960s and early 1970s. Equally important to this growth of the public's awareness of his work were the numerous workshops and demonstrations he conducted throughout the United States and Europe between 1968 and 1975. He has continued this time-consuming practice to the present, with a recent workshop and exhibition in Japan (1980). The workshop-exhibition phenomenon saw its greatest popularity during the 1970s, spawning numerous regional permanent workshop centers. Perhaps the most far-reaching manifestations of this effort to expose the public and younger photographers to the ideas of leaders of photography are the annual conferences of the National Society for Photographic Education, held in a different region of the United States each year, and the Rencontres Internationales de la Photographie, held each summer in Arles, France. It is important to note, however, that this method of promoting artists and educating the public is far from new: Ansel Adams has been leading his own workshop in Yosemite National Park since the late 1930s. It is worth mentioning that Uelsmann's experience from 1970 on has shown a strong similarity to that of Ansel Adams with respect to acceptance by both his peers and the general public. Both artists are indefatigable teachers of their own special brand of craft and special vision, and while their imagery may differ greatly, the content of their work universally appeals to emotions and a desire for idealism. Most important, neither Uelsmann nor Adams has sought selective audiences; both have engaged admirers in many and varied quarters. Neither has been thwarted by intermittent negative criticism from the rapidly growing and sometimes restless photography community. In Uelsmann's case, such criticism has come only rarely, and primarily from a few critics who seem to feel that the weight of a large body of work with a style changing only subtly is somehow oppressive. The impatience of such critics is most often accompanied by a zeal for new manifestations of the avant-garde and little credence is placed in the value of an informed perspective forged from years of consistency. The chief vehicles for criticism (newspapers, magazines, photography tabloids) demonstrate that art criticism, at its best, is a form of finely crafted journalism; at its worst, it is biased editorialism. When criticism takes the essay form, it is less of either, and becomes more a philosophy of art. Perhaps a better name for art critic would be "art analyst." (I admit to a prejudiced view of art criticism, subscribing to the idea expressed by Etienne Gilson in his essay "Painters and the Talking

World." In it he refutes the idea that criticism is a necessary requisite for a field to reach maturity: "Literary critics create literature about literature; they write about writings. But art critics do not write music about music, nor do they paint about painting; they express themselves in words about an art that is not an art of words."[29] Essays on an artist's work are entirely another matter, for in this form of writing there is no pretense of judgmental authority.)

In 1967 *Infinity* (the journal of the American Society of Magazine Photographers) published a portfolio of eleven photographs by Uelsmann with an essay by William Parker, written before the author's seminal essay in *Aperture* that same year. This publication reflects two important facts. First, the editor's inviting Parker to write about Uelsmann indicated an interest in his work outside the narrow world of fine art photography; *Infinity* traditionally sought to give exposure to artists outside its own strongly commercial ranks, but at the same time its editors required of its subjects a certain level of recognition. Second, since Parker did not know Uelsmann personally at the time, his approach to the work was fresh and spontaneous, and also could not have been influenced by Uelsmann's charismatic personality or by the photographer's own assessment of his work. Parker's essay was a clear, concisely written explanation of the photographs in terms of symbolist art, noting Uelsmann's concept of post-visualization and citing precedents to reinforce the author's interpretation of the work. He focused on both the believable nonreality that made Uelsmann's work distinctive and on the intensity of recognition Uelsmann was receiving: "It is because of the medium of photography that Uelsmann's work is fundamentally believable. Simplistic as this may sound, it is hardly conceivable that his work would elicit such intense attention on the basis of unique imagery or composition alone."[30] The essay planted seeds of understanding and appreciation of the photographs in terms of an informed psychological approach, but stopped short of attributing psychological principles to the work itself. More important, Parker did not once refer to "Surrealism." This mistaken association seems to have arisen more from assumptions made by the popular press and the public than from the perceptions of those who wrote in depth about Uelsmann. In any case, the exposure in *Infinity* was probably less significant than that in subsequent articles, except for the broadening of Uelsmann's audience.

A year later (1968), A. D. Coleman reviewed Parker's more complex essay in *Aperture* ("Uelsmann's Unitary Reality") for New York's *Village Voice*. Again, Uelsmann's audience was broadening. While Coleman admitted to not understanding the essay, he credited it with being "the first of its kind I've ever seen devoted to a photographer's work." He also gave Uelsmann's work the most glowing review it had yet received. Speaking of the photographs, he said,

*They remind me of nothing any other photographer has ever done. (Magritte is the only artist whose "symbolic syntax"—as Parker puts it—has had an obvious influence on Uelsmann.) I truly don't know how to describe them, but they stay in your head, haunting and perplexing. Their intent is specifically non-verbal—one of the reasons I find Parker's essay unnecessary; Uelsmann is not trying to "tell a story," as Henry P. Robinson did, but to portray and evoke moments of dream-trance-subconscious awareness through visual, not verbal, imagery. When he succeeds (which is often), I find myself unconcerned with questions of technique and Is-this-photography, caught up instead by an elusive memory from my inner past. As I said, you can't argue with success.*[31]

Coleman's positive reaction to Uelsmann's photography signaled that the time was right for the photography world to look upon this new work with keener interest. Perhaps it was important that it was a *publication* on Uelsmann's photographs rather than an exhibition that was being reviewed. Rightly or wrongly, a book brings distinction to a photographer's work and remains a major mark of approval to the general public and peers alike. (Frederick Sommer once related to me a remark made by Max Ernst: "An exhibition without documentation [a publication] isn't worth the time it takes to put it up.") Publications reviewed by major personalities in prominent newspapers have a doubly energizing effect. Uelsmann is, and always has been, aware of this process, although he insulates himself against negative reviews by paraphrasing a comment he attributed to Man Ray: "One should not read reviews; just measure them."

By the time of Coleman's review, Uelsmann's photographs were being included in important national group exhibitions like *Photography as Printmaking* at the Museum of Modern Art and *Persistence of Vision* at George Eastman House. His one-man exhibitions were also appearing throughout the country (from the Massachusetts Institute of Technology to the Minneapolis Institute of Arts and the University of Oregon Museum of Art). From this point the list of his exhibitions is as distinguished and extensive as any artist could aspire to.

Almost as if he needed to remind himself that success as an artist could not be achieved in the pages of tabloids and magazines, the next few articles that Uelsmann wrote emphasized what he refers to as the humanistic awareness an artist must have for his work and self. In a short tribute to Wynn Bullock in *Modern Photography* in 1970, Uelsmann wrote about Bullock's photographs in such a way that his own name could easily have been substituted for Bullock's without misleading the reader. An excerpt from this piece reveals the influence that Bullock — one of his "silver heroes" — had on Uelsmann:

*You cannot remain indifferent to Bullock's photographs. They are evocative and provocative, eventually leading one from a world of perceptive consciousness into a world of visual and mental involvement. They are images for the mind as well as the eye. The viewer becomes a participant, for the photographs address themselves primarily to his inventive consciousness and less to his ability to recall. In discovering ways of relating to his photographs we can learn much about ourselves.*

*There are few artists today as sensible to themselves and their surroundings. As a result his images are closer to the "source," to those inner vibrations that cause a man to become an image-maker. They contain evidence of a deep humanistic concern and one can readily sense within them his stated desire "to trace the hidden roots of man deeply imbedded in basic nature."*[32]

The idea that nature can be pictorially manipulated to become a metaphor for human feelings is not new to photography or to other visual arts. Yet each time an artist discovers the possibility for himself, a new set of internal needs is funneled into a vortex formed of changing environment, cultural shifts, and different social circumstances, all whirling in a complex around the artist himself. The resulting works are inescapably unique. It is during such fragile moments of personal discovery that the difference between influence and inspiration is established. A strong influence reverberates—if only superficially—in trends, while with inspiration the aesthetic continuum is veiled with individual detail.

The humanistic concern that Uelsmann perceives in Bullock's photographs is also at work in his own. He uses the word "humanistic" to describe works of art that are based in human emotions and values, whether symbolized by nature or other subjects. Within his use of the word is also subsumed a concern for spiritual and aesthetic values related to the process of creativity (as opposed to concern for gain and recognition). His use of, and interest in, the word is a mark of rebellion against the search for success in the marketplace and technical accomplishment for its own sake. It is a rare photograph by Uelsmann that does not include either some natural or human element, and by far the larger part of his imagery is an entanglement of the two. Although this predominance of humanistic concern may not be totally planned, the undercurrent of its effect is intense enough to have caused him to devote a lecture paper to the subject in 1971. The Royal Photographic Society of Great Britain invited him to give the Fourth Bertram Cox Memorial lecture in London; the subject Uelsmann chose for this lecture, "Some Humanistic Considerations of Photography," grew out of his desire to keep his rapidly growing popularity in perspective and to make concrete, for himself, his aesthetic attitudes:

*It is my feeling that today, photography, along with most other art media, has become product oriented. Our thoughts and actions throughout the entire process are dominated by our desire to produce a given result. The goal has become far more important than the process. An attitude more respectful to the process can perhaps best be illustrated by the analogy of the symphony orchestra, which does not play to reach the end of a composition, but for which each moment of sound is of immediate and continuing significance. As with the orchestra, the celebration we call photography is also a myriad of moments and experiences, each with the possibilities of immediate and sustained significance. It is important to realize that all aspects of the photographic process carry the seeds of revelation.*[33]

This quotation conveys the essence of the lecture, which was aimed in part at the demechanization of the technical side of photography, at least in terms of the artist's attitude toward process. The thrust of the lecture was an extension of Uelsmann's post-visualization concept, an admonishment to photographers for complacently following the dicta of pre-visualization and treating the process of making the print as a mechanical craft dealing with a fait accompli. It also stressed, as the quotation reveals, Uelsmann's view that each photograph is an end in itself to be enjoyed independent of a known corpus of work. It was a call for reining in professional ambition, especially when desires for attention, acclaim, and other presumed rewards eroded the depth of the artist's feeling—his humanistic concern—for the creative process. Uelsmann was not proselytizing, but speaking from personal experience of the pressures he had begun to feel from the demands of the public arena, and the dangers they presented to his own work. He faced the dilemma of making decisions to satisfy either the marketplace or his own aesthetic needs; the two are rarely compatible, especially when of equal intensity, for long. Uelsmann suggested that an appreciation of all aspects of the photographic process was the only attitude that allowed one to remain in "human" contact with one's art. Without this, one manufactured rather than created.

Focusing on these concerns can help to clarify two aspects of Uelsmann's work that some viewers have found disconcerting: his use of variations of the same image; and the seeming immutability of his style over the years. With respect to the first (see, for example, figures 29 and 30), Uelsmann has written:

*Time and again people ask me which image I like best, and I try to avoid this sort of qualitative distinction. Sometimes it's very clear as to which works better, but . . . I think that they are equal yet different.*

*A point I want to bring up here is that it's hard to know when you're printing an image what long range value it will have. I've had an image occur in the darkroom and thought, "There's a real winner," and I've printed twenty of them. The next day I wonder why I did it. Then there are times when I've made one print and a week later I had to go back and print more because I liked it so much.*

*One of the hazards of working this way for a long time is that you begin to pre-visualize your post-visualization. If I start working it out too much, I set blocks for myself. I go out on a*

Figure 29. *1967*            Figure 30. *1967*

*limb to be more casual, because I like the idea of letting the medium have a say in the image as it evolves.*[34]

Such variations, then, are not a matter of indecision, or a means of working up to a final image. Rather, they form a process by which Uelsmann explores a single theme, a concept we readily accept in music, and one that is no less valid for the visual arts. Additionally, the different versions allow Uelsmann to flow with the "syntax" of the medium. The joy of allowing a medium certain freedom to express its own inherent vernacular — to push paint around, as it were — is an aspect of the respect and love all artists have for their preferred materials. The fact that Uelsmann finds value in each of his photographs, independent of all others, is also pertinent. The viewer should do the same, for each image, no matter how similar to another, is in effect played in a different key, striking different chords within us.

The uneasiness about Uelsmann's unchanging style should be buried with the recognition that the very constancy of his approach and vision is its greatest strength (figures 31 and 32). It is also wrong to assume that because his photographs possess consistent autographic qualities (style) the work has not changed. It is curious that Uelsmann's photography is criticized for consistency when in other media consistency of style and depth of aesthetic intent are praised as qualities that mark artists as innovators and masters of movements. Perhaps the best arguments against the merits of such complaints are the sources of such criticism, which has generally been expressed in photography tabloids by writers who seem to be trying too hard to place Uelsmann's work within whatever model is the

Figure 31. *1963*

Figure 32. *1975*

contemporary trend. But such personal misdirections aside, the question remains as to the viability of Uelsmann's continuing in the way he has always worked — that is, with multiple printing and enigmatic imagery.

One of the most lucid critical reviews of Uelsmann's photography (one which showed that the author was in no way troubled by the matter of unchanging style) was written by A. D. Coleman for *The New York Times* of Sunday, January 3, 1971. While the review was occasioned by a major two-hundred-print retrospective exhibition of Uelsmann's photography at the Philadelphia Museum of Art, it covered a great many more critical issues than is typical of newspaper reviews. The questions addressed by Coleman were typical, rather, of his style of criticism. The positive and firm nature of his observations left little likelihood that the public's interest in Uelsmann would flag:

*Signposts along the road to widespread acceptance of Uelsmann's art have been appearing at an increasing rate over the past few years. Aside from the pervasiveness of his influence . . . and the frequency with which his images are shown, published, and discussed, two of the most significant pieces of recent photographic criticism (William E. Parker's extended essay in* Aperture *13:3 and John L. Ward's monograph, "The Criticism of Photography as Art: The Photographs of Jerry Uelsmann," published by the University of Florida Press) are either devoted to or based on Uelsmann's photographs. . . . And, if all that is not enough to convince the skeptics, then the overwhelming Uelsmann retrospective which opened at the Philadelphia Museum of Art . . . should certainly end the argument.*

Coleman described the contents of the exhibition as a collection of "creative imagery as cogent, as consistent, and as durable as any being made today." He addressed the issue of the multiple-printing technique historically, in relation to Robinson and Rejlander, suggesting that the failure of the earlier work was due not to technique, but rather to content, for the nineteenth-century artists imitated the worst in literature and painting of the period. This was the first time that Uelsmann's controversial technique-style had been discussed openly and directly in the face of the "pre-visualization" aesthetic, which still dominated the photography art world. In fact, Coleman's comments, in conjunction with Uelsmann's influence as a nonpurist, may have played a major role in the explosion of manipulated and experimental photographs by younger photographers of the 1970s. Equally important and well-known sources of influence at that time, like the work and teaching of Robert Heinecken and Nathan Lyons's Visual Studies Workshop, reinforced the aesthetic stance that Uelsmann represented. Coleman publicly opened the door for the revival of historical and neglected techniques. He invoked the Photo-Secessionists' dictum that the end result was the only fair basis for judgment when he wrote in his review: "Since techniques neither die (unless by improvement beyond recognition) nor carry any internal rightness or wrongness, it [the multiple-printing technique] simply waited . . . for an esthetic it would fit." Coleman's review, which was more about Uelsmann's aesthetic than his exhibition, went on to discuss the personal nature of the imagery, and the viewer's link to the photographs through his or her subconscious. The subconscious thus became, and remains largely to date, the accepted means by which viewer and critic alike project their interpretations onto Uelsmann's photography. Such personalization, however, contradicts the fact that Uelsmann's photographs are *his* personal record, rather than the viewer's. To allow the viewer this easy way out may in the long run prove a great handicap to a thorough understanding of the work.

"Born of his hand under the guidance of his mind, paintings are made in the image and likeness of the painter," wrote Gilson in *Painting and Reality*. In this perceptive book with unique insights into the relationship of artist-to-audience-to-critic, Gilson also states that works of art are not beautiful because they please us, but that they please us because they are beautiful.[35] The same might be said in reference to Uelsmann's imagery. The mystery of his images is not relevant to our subconscious, but our subconscious is stimulated because his imagery is mysterious. For this reason, as has been suggested earlier, Uelsmann's photographs should be considered in terms of visual mythology; that is, as events and creations outside ourselves. Our reactions should be the same as with any other non-narrative art form; pleasure when our minds and vision are pleased, and reflection when symbols stir our curiosity. To demand consideration of this kind is not unusual. In a recent review of a new painting by James Rosenquist, art critic John Ashbery wrote in *Newsweek* (February 9, 1981): "As usual, the juxtaposition of images—slices of bacon floating in interstellar space, a woman's face separating to reveal skeins of colored electrical wire behind it — and the bewildering shifts in scale and perspective are important less for themselves than for their contiguity." Ashbery could easily have been describing a photograph by Uelsmann. The remainder of Ashbery's comment offers an even closer analogy to Uelsmann's imagery. "If one stops to 'read' the painting, one could end up misunderstanding it. Is the fact that the woman is apparently being penetrated by a metal shaft, or that her flesh might be turning into bacon, meant as some kind of comment on the human condition? Probably not. It makes more sense to see it all as a moment of collision in which the impact, rather than the objects producing it, is what counts."

During the several years following the Philadelphia exhibition, Uelsmann's photographs became even more diverse in terms of subject. His technique grew in sophistication to the point that his playfulness with the technique itself began to lighten the drama which characterized so much of the earlier work. Manipulations of space, scale, and perspective, which had interested him at the beginning of his career as devices in the service of the construction of an image, now became central concerns of his aesthetic. These formal elements, among others, became the objects of exploration themselves, making an even more complex imagery, which still fused recognizable subjects in unpredictable ways. The humor, enigma, absurdity, and fantasy all remained, but a new geometry controlled their presentation. Where earlier Uelsmann had erased the boundaries of "reality" for photography, he was now fracturing the boundaries of the frame of reference itself. Before, his images were as if on a stage, with the illusion protected by the four "walls" of the photograph. The stage remained in this new work, but the viewer was invited to enter on it and exchange pure illusion for a participation in the act itself. In 1978, at the beginning of his cooperation with the author to produce this mongraph, Uelsmann wrote:

*The term "recent work" has different connotations for me now at mid-career than it had earlier in my visual evolution. I feel strongly that my growth continues. Recent growth is less involved with the expansion of my technical vocabulary and more concerned with the evocative subtleties involved in the use of that vocabulary. I sense an ever-increasing rapport with, and trust of, the role of the pre-conscious and play in my personal imagistic process.*[36]

# 1976-1981

Since 1975 Uelsmann's photography has been increasingly exhibited and published internationally, with one-man exhibitions far outnumbering group and thematic shows. To say that he remains prolific in this yearly harvest of images begins to sound redundant. One might say that this is the nature of all photographers, but references to their productivity are usually based on their caches of silent, unused negatives and prints. In Uelsmann's case, his productivity is not measured by the number of works on a contact sheet, but by the numbers of new works appearing from exhibition to exhibition. Keeping up with this flow presents problems for critics and the public alike. Each new review of Uelsmann's work seems to result in a look back, as if from retinal retention of his past work. The desire for change that fires our enthusiasm for the arts makes us, paradoxically, look over our shoulders, rather than straight ahead. It is a strange kind of blindness, like driving backward and expecting the unfolding landscape that reveals where we have been to tell us where we are going. The changes that have taken place in Uelsmann's work during the last few years are subtle and must be viewed with an appreciation of that subtlety. A comparison of these works with those of a decade ago reveals a preponderance of similar motifs and poetic interrelationships. This is surely a major strength in his work; however, we must be willing to set the past aside for a moment in order to try to see works of the present in the present. This does not lessen the value of looking over one's shoulder to obtain perspective. But the function is different for each approach: in looking back, we are like accountants; in confining ourselves to the present, we are like investors. A brief look at reviews of Uelsmann's photography since 1975 reveals both approaches. Additionally, almost all of these reviews clearly accept without question Uelsmann's stature as an artist of major influence.

John Szarkowski, in his controversial book *Mirrors and Windows: American Photography since 1960*, was more reserved in his description of Uelsmann's influence in photography, yet even his comments were laced with adjectives portending canonization: "Jerry N. Uelsmann's fanciful, intricate, and technically brilliant montages have been broadly influential, but not widely followed. His pictures persuaded half the photography students of the sixties that manipulated photographs could be both philosophically acceptable and aesthetically rewarding, but few of those students adopted Uelsmann's fey, Edwardian surrealism, or his very demanding technical system."[37] Szarkowski was correct in saying that Uelsmann's work was not "widely followed," in the sense of imitation. Also, his description of Uelsmann's photographs as "fey" and "Edwardian" is not surprising, in light of Szarkowski's enthusiasm for the work of photographers like Garry Winogrand and William Eggleston, whose works appear antiseptically rational next to Uelsmann's.

In addition to published reviews, the commercial gallery system also has had an impact on Uelsmann's reputation, and on photography in general, over the past decade. Throughout most of the twentieth century artists have depended to a great extent upon the exposure and sales generated by the commercial galleries. It is an undeniable fact that a "reputation" is not fully established until a consistent sales record has been achieved. For those who find this thought repugnant, it should be noted that, historically, commercial galleries have been as effective as, and perhaps more adventurous than, the great majority of museums and art centers in promoting contemporary art. It is a fact that for the most part the nonprofit institutions depend upon the commercial gallery system to seek out and bestow approval upon artists before the institutions purchase their works. Even if occasionally this system is circumvented, the results are not necessarily beneficial to the reputations of the artists, who lose the promotion that is provided by the commercial galleries. Newspapers and specialized art magazines rely upon the prolific activities of galleries to fill their pages (as well as finance them through advertising). Collectors desire the stamp of approval from a reputable gallery and only rarely deal exclusively with the artist. The effect of the gallery system is naturally two-edged, since there are less attractive aspects, with the inherent dangers of "packaging" and exploitation at the top of the list. Nevertheless, the system is effective and has played an important role in broadening the public's exposure to, and acceptance of, photography since the late 1960s.

There is a long list of commercial galleries that have shown and promoted Uelsmann's work, the earliest being the Carl Siembab Gallery in Boston in 1969. However, the one that has been the most consistent and effective promoter of Uelsmann's photography is the Witkin Gallery in New York, with exhibitions in 1972, 1975, 1977, and 1981. How is this pertinent to a discussion of Uelsmann's recent work? These galleries did not define their exhibitions in retrospective terms, but were constant forums for the exposure of his newest images. Witkin's exhibitions alone could have kept the public up to date on the evolution of Uelsmann's photography. Museums do not have the flexibility or the responsibility to present individual artists' works repeatedly every year or so. Their obligations are much

Figure 33. *1980*

broader. As a result of gallery exhibitions, however, major critical instruments like *The New York Times* are given the opportunity to keep abreast of Uelsmann's development.

It is, therefore, especially meaningful when Hilton Kramer, art critic of *The New York Times*, applauds Uelsmann's most recent work, exhibited at the Witkin Gallery during January 1981 (figure 33):

*Poetic invention abounds, and there is little repetition from image to image in a copious production. . . . Someone once compared the formal organization of his work to the characteristic divisions of space we find in the paintings of Mark Rothko and Adolph Gottlieb, and he has surely looked at a lot of abstract art. From it he has achieved an enviable mastery of a space that, though often crowded with visual incident, is always perfectly legible and coherent. Even where the imagery is hermetic, its details are never obscure or confused.*[38]

Kramer's comments reflect a change in critical approach to the work; as discussed earlier, there has been more than enough of critics' personal interpretations of Uelsmann's imagery offered for public consumption. As his work has become more obviously syntactical in the relationship of subject matter to formal elements, a need has developed for the viewer to respond more objectively and "visually." Kramer makes a major point concerning the subtlety of the change that has taken place in the new work, remarking on the special interest of the pictures based on Uelsmann's recent travels in Japan. "This experience seems to have made his pictures somewhat leaner and more austere than they have been. The technique employed in these pictures . . . remains painstaking and complex, but the results are often simpler and more direct." This observation goes to the heart of Uelsmann's current work and it is no accident that the formal elements that lend the simplicity are themselves imaginary. Geometric form—spheres, cubes, and other volumetric shapes—have increasingly become the "subjects" of central focus. These objects float, metamorphose, and alter the context of the environment—all themes that occur throughout Uelsmann's imagery.

Uelsmann's variations on a theme are not restricted to different versions of closely related individual photographs. As was briefly mentioned earlier, motifs that he has consistently explored can be conveniently divided into different areas of visual concern. These divisions contain variations that can be studied laterally (across the range of his contemporaneous works) or historically (by tracing their evolution through his oeuvre). While each division may be dominated by a particular motif (such as the floating object), individual images within that division nearly always incorporate, even if in subdued form, motifs from other divisions. Among the dominant motifs easily recognized are the following: floating objects, metamorphosing forms — architectural or human — sensual nudes, room interiors, environmental insets, windows and doors, material transmutation, and references to classical antiquity or other art historical periods. Details that commonly convey these themes are rocks, water, clouds, trees, hands, eyes, mirrors, and flora in abundance. Visual and formal devices used to structure the variations include accentuated foreground scale, extreme linear perspective, varied focus, positive-negative reversal, drawing, and collaging.

Uelsmann has used more broadly based, subjective definitions to categorize these broad areas of visual concern, such as the predicament of Man, nature-energy, embedded figures, dream moments, and portraits. These phrases are about as close as he has ever come to interpreting his own work. His terms allow all motif categories to overlap and provide an order for viewer synthesis. This should not be mistaken for an invitation to make specific personalized interpretations. The excesses of that form of appreciation are only compounded by the vagueness of Uelsmann's definitions.

These fundamental aspects of Uelsmann's photographs are discussed here rather than at the beginning of this study so as to avoid prejudicing the reader, to allow him to look at the work from a strictly objective point of view. The photographs should be enjoyed for their evocative poetry and visual mythology before all other considerations. Joan Murray, photography editor of *Artweek*, has expressed this sentiment particularly well:

*I think of Uelsmann's work as seductive — beguiling and enticing all of our senses. His work is so explicitly human, so close to emotional nerve endings, that once one is drawn into Uelsmann's imagery, the response will occur again and again. . . . If a certain rigidity of spirit resists being beguiled and led into deepest fantasies, then the viewer will turn away. Those open to the mysteries of his images become the admirers of his work.*[39]

Color photography in all its manifestations, from various hand-manipulation techniques to straight manufacturing processes, dominates the scene today. Yet, typical of Uelsmann's self-assurance and independence, he has not been tempted to join such a movement. The word "movement" is used guardedly, since the current flurry of interest in color may turn out to be no more than a fad or brief revival of a previous cycle. At least once before in the history of the medium, color temporarily commanded the attention of serious photographic artists. The advent of the autochrome at the turn of the century invited limited experimentation, which was extended by various monochrome colorations of the Photo-Secession (gum-bichromate, gravure). This and other less important collective attempts eventually gave way, however, to a return to an essentially black-and-white medium. The issue of "color" photography today is different, in any case, since it applies to processes related to photography (collage, offset lithography, multimedia, and so on) as well as to photographs, and all are accepted with equity under the same umbrella.

In a sense, Uelsmann anticipated the current exploration of color almost a decade before its flowering in the 1970s. In 1968 he produced a dozen or so images that were selectively toned in vibrant hues, resulting in works of two and three colors. While these were colored images rather than color photographs per se, their appearance was more analogous to process color than to color produced by hand-manipulation techniques. There is little doubt that Uelsmann's isolated experiment with color was probably more an outgrowth of the latent influence of Henry Holmes Smith than a serious grappling with a color aesthetic. Although some of these images are in a way the most provocative of Uelsmann's work from the period (plates 52–54), he decided that color offered little advantage in pursuing his aesthetic interests, and he was not convinced that adapting color systems to his elaborate technique would be more than a gimmick. The high cost of color processing may also have played a role in his decision to abandon color after 1968; today, however, the situation is quite different, with the photography market and several competing color systems encouraging the exploration of color, but Uelsmann continues to work only in black and white. He was also concerned about the permanence of the toned prints and did not want to gamble on the eventual outcome. His commitment to craftsmanship is all-encompassing and a strong dose of the puritan ethic would not allow him to leave this worry to collectors of his work. This problem is unresolved for color photography in general and remains a volatile issue for today's colorists, as well as those who wish to own and preserve such work. In the end, however, the final arbiters of the color issue will be the artists themselves, making decisions based primarily on aesthetic issues, as Uelsmann has done.

Always powerfully attracted to the black-and-white process, Uelsmann says that he continues to be intrigued by the possibilities of the darkroom, which are now greater than ever. Having developed a very specific and complex vocabulary over the past twenty-five years, he has become more patient with, if still immune to, what he calls "fashion" photography. Where in years past his anxiety level might have risen when each new voguish concentration of the medium flared, today that "doubt," as he used to refer to it, has been resolved into an insatiable desire to refine his vocabulary into a universal dialect. He believes that by striving to develop nuances in what is an unquestionably mature vision, he will add depth to it. The wisdom of that conviction has been borne out by many of history's great artists. The work of Monet, for example, provides ample evidence of the depth one artist was able to achieve in his art by obsessive refinement; his last works carry the aesthetic genes of his early impressionism, but they also have an energy of impasto and brushstroke that anticipates abstract expressionism. The changes we are beginning to see in Uelsmann's work, with a "leaner," more stark imagery, particularly in the geometric forms (figure 34), suggest that it is evolving into a stage that will be as great a contrast to the work that immediately preceded it as were the photographs of the fifties to those of the sixties.

One could discuss Uelsmann's current work in the context of numerous fronts that proliferate in the field today, such as marked photography, topographical objectivism, and conceptual banality, among others. Yet to do so would be akin to using a kind of Nielson system to rate the effectiveness of his aesthetic in relation to those of popular headliners. Also, a lack of cohesion within the various fronts themselves would make for a rather convoluted exercise that in the end would be fruitless. Even the unfocused preoccupation with color which has blanketed the field is not an appropriate point of departure, since Uelsmann has decidedly declined to join in. However, it is safe to say that no artist is capa-

Figure 34. *1980*

ble of working totally outside the perceptions (social, cultural, political, and environmental) of his or her time. And in that regard, the astute observer can find aspects of many of the fronts metaphorically embraced in Uelsmann's work. The volumetric forms dominating his work since 1979 can be seen as a sympathetic reaction to the generally antipictorial bias of most photography today. Also evident in his work is the seventies' deemphasis of photographic purity, which is most conspicuously manifested by marking on the photograph itself.

This does not mean that the ontological nature of his iconography is disappearing, but rather that its romanticism is being tamed. The idealistic, passionate, mythological character of Uelsmann's imagery will probably never disappear, because he is intrinsically an idealist pitting humanism against mysticism, the believable against the unbelievable.

# Portfolio

1954–1966

1. *1956*

2. *1959 Homage to Thoreau*

3. 1958

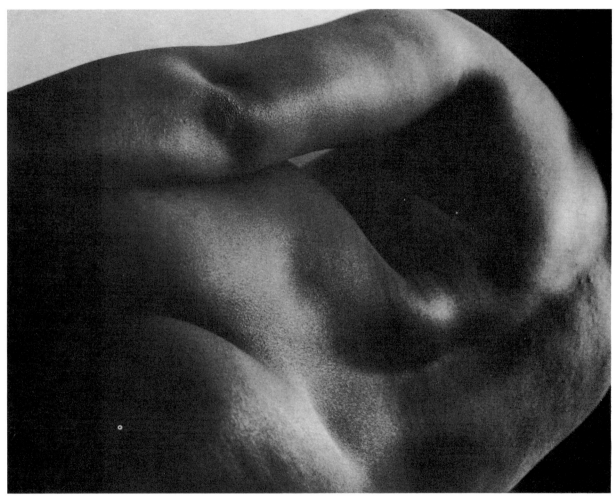

4. 1959

5. 1960

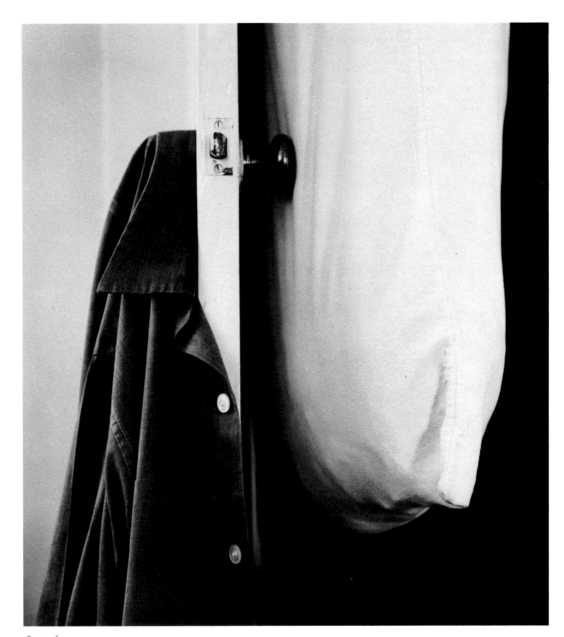

6. *1960*

7. 1959

8. *1955*

9. *1960*

10. *1958*

11. *1960*

12. *1960*

13. *1960*

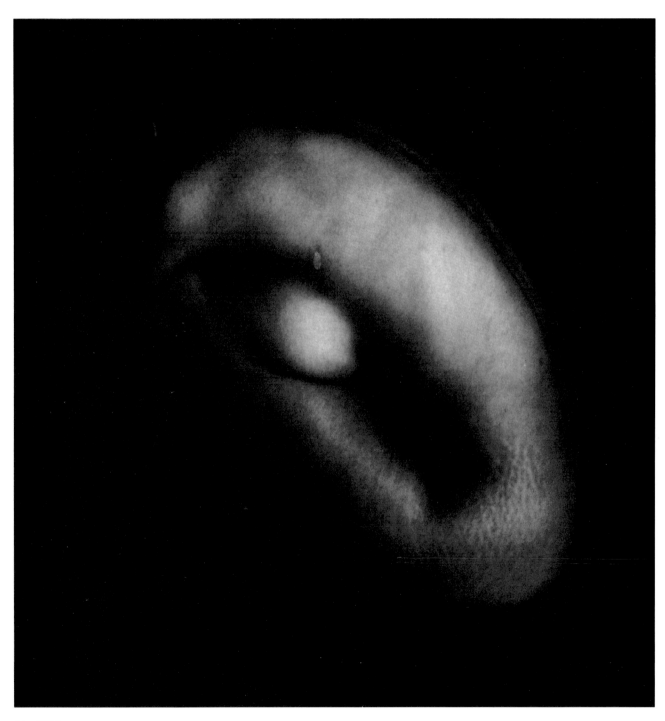

14. 1955

15. *1960*

16. *1961*

17. *1961*

18. *1961 Fallen Warriors*

19. *1961*

20. *1961 Symbolic Mutation*

21. *1962*

22. 1963

23. 1963

24. *1962*

25. 1962

26. 1964

27. 1963

28. *1963*

29. *1963*

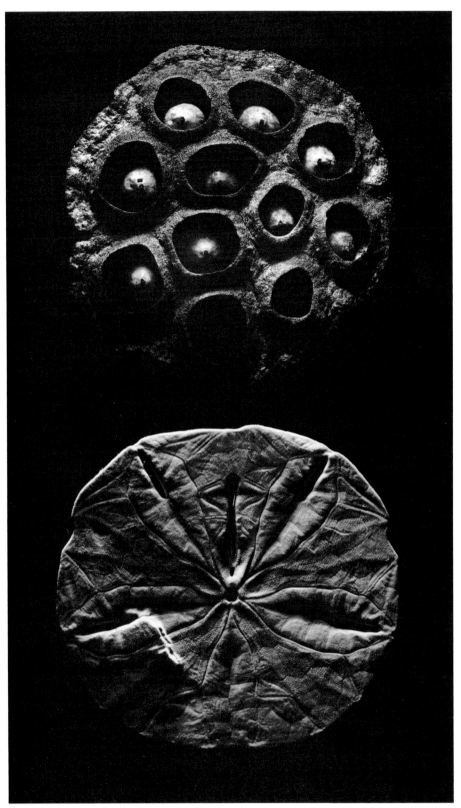

30. 1963

31. *1964–1968*

32. 1963 Myth of the Tree

33. 1965

34. *1964 Marilynn and the Sheep*

35. *1964*

*36. 1964 My Angel*

37. *1963 Room No. 1*

38. *1964 Conjecture of a Time*

39. *1966 Undiscovered Self*

40. 1966

41. *1965 Magritte's Touchstone*

42. 1965

43. 1966

44. *1966*

1967–1975

45. *1967 Sky House*

46. *1967*

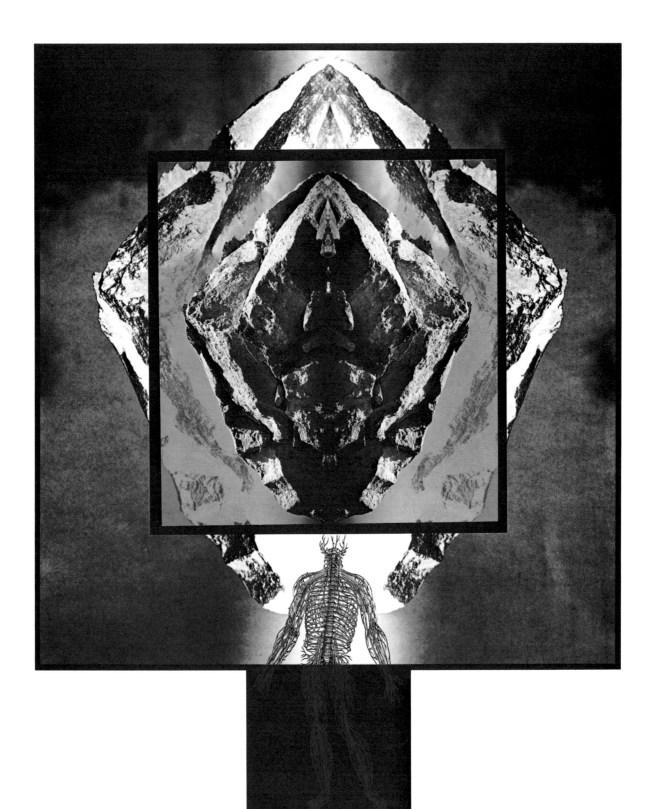

47. *1968*

48. *1967 Small Woods Where I Met Myself*

49. *1968*

50. *1970*

51. *1970 Totemic Aspen*

52. *1968 Turtle Blessing* (toning experiment)

53. *1968* (toning experiment)

54. *1968* (toning experiment)

55. *1969 Point Lobos*

56. 1968

57. 1969

58. 1968

59. *1973 Place of Several Mysteries*

60. *1971*

61. *1971*

62. *1972*

63. *1971*

64. *1969*

65. *1975*

66. *1973 Aaron*

67. *1974 The Lady and the Tiger*

68. *1975*

69. *1973 Simultaneous Implications*

70. *1974 French Bedroom*

71. 1973

72. 1974

73. 1975

74. 1975

75. 1974

76. 1975 *Babel*

77. 1974

78. 1971

79. *1975*

80. *1975*

81. *1974*

82. *1975*

83. 1975

1976–1981

84. *1976*

85. *1976*

86. *1976*

87. *1976 The Gifts of St. Ann*

88. *1977*

89. *1976*

90. *1978 Diane*

91. *1976 Bicentennial Image*

92. 1976

93. *1977*

94. *1978 Animal Dreams*

95. *1976*

96. *1976*

97. *1976*

98. *1978*

99. *1978*

100. *1977*

101. *1976*

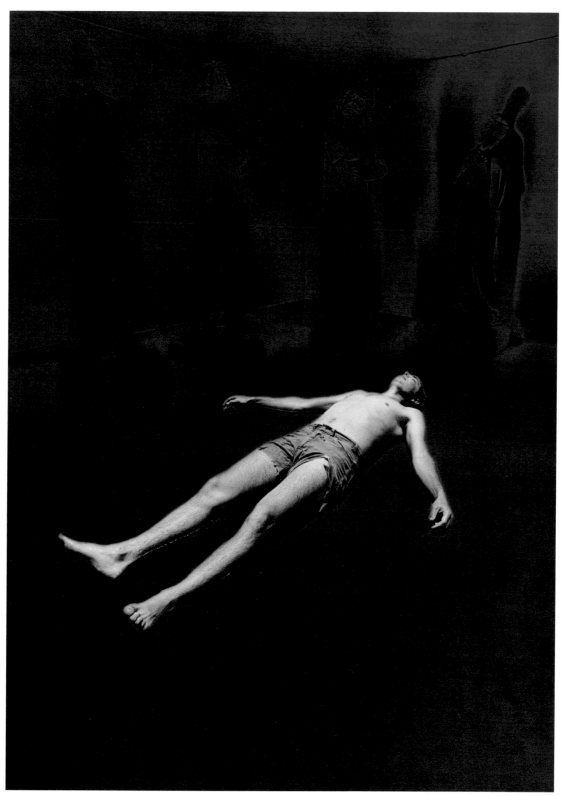

102. *1977*

103. *1977*

104. *1978*

105. *1977*

106. *1978*

107. *1978 Animus/Anima, Self-Portrait*

108. *1977*

109. *1977*

110. *1978*

111. *1978*

112. *1978*

113. *1979*

114. *1981*

115. *1980*

116. *1979*

117. *1979*

118. *1979*

119. *1979*

120. *1981*

121. *1981*

122. *1979*

123. *1979*

124. *1980*

125. *1981*

126. *1981*

127. 1980

128. *1981*

129. *1981*

130. *1981*

131. *1981*

132. *1981*

133. *1980*

134. 1980

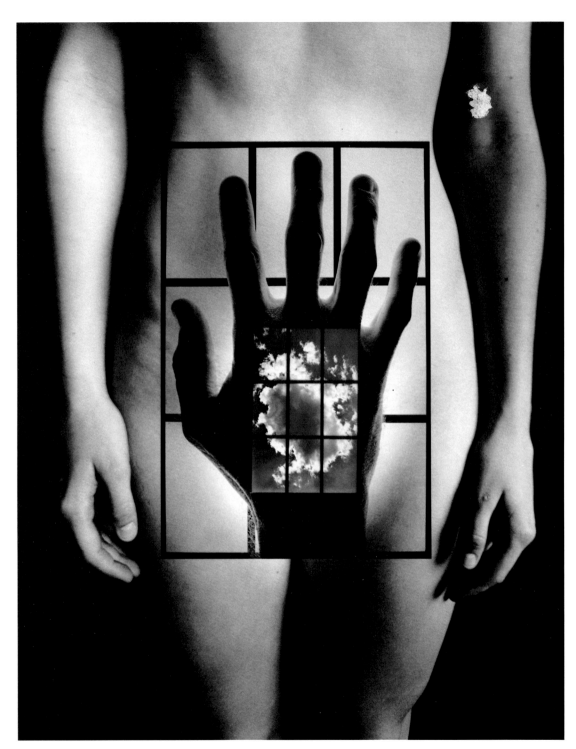

135. *1980*

136. *1980*

137. *1980*

138. *1980*

139. *1981*

140. *1980*

# Notes

Epigraph, page 9: from *Nietzsche*, Walter Kaufmann, ed. (New York: The Viking Press, 1975), p. 17.

1. Bunnell, *Jerry Uelsmann: Silver Meditations*, Introduction (not paginated).

2. Quoted in H. B. Cotterill, *A History of Art* (London: George G. Harrap and Co. Ltd., 1924), vol. II, p. 360.

3. Quoted from draft manuscript of Uelsmann manifesto dated January 1962.

4. "Some Humanistic Considerations of Photography," *The Photographic Journal* 3:4 (April 1971), p. 166.

5. "Post-Visualization," manuscript (1967), p. 6.

6. Letter to author, September 1, 1979.

7. Aaron Siskind, from a statement delivered as part of a lecture on his work at the Rencontres Internationales de la Photographie, Arles, France (July 1979): ". . . as the vocabulary of photography has been extended, the emphasis of meaning has shifted — shifted from what the world looks like to what we feel about the world and what we want the world to mean."

8. "Some Humanistic Considerations of Photography," pp. 168, 170.

9. Henry Holmes Smith, reader's report, November 28, 1969, for University of Florida Press on John L. Ward, *The Criticism of Photography As Art: The Photographs of Jerry Uelsmann*.

10. "Some Humanistic Considerations of Photography," p. 167.

11. Ibid., pp. 167, 172.

12. From original draft for *Darkroom*, Eleanor Lewis, ed. (1977), p. 3.

13. Bunnell, *Aperture* 15:4 (1970), introduction (not paginated).

14. Letter to Henry Holmes Smith, October 16, 1960, Archive of Center for Creative Photography, University of Arizona.

15. "Some Humanistic Considerations of Photography," p. 169.

16. From original manifesto (January 1962); reprinted in full on pp. 35–38.

17. "How Jerry Uelsmann Creates His Multiple Images," *Popular Photography* (January 1977).

18. See Charles T. Tart, ed., *Altered States of Consciousness* (New York: Doubleday Anchor Books, 1972), pp. 465–469.

19. *The Photographic Journal* 3:3 (March 1971), p. 118.

20. The total of 15,000 copies is an estimated number sold to date. It is estimated as well that the *Aperture* issue with Peter Bunnell's essay has sold over 25,000 copies to date.

21. *Silver Meditations*.

22. "The Photography of Jerry N. Uelsmann," *Contemporary Photographer*, Lee Lockwood, ed., 5:1 (Winter 1964), p. 48.

23. "Some Humanistic Considerations of Photography," p. 170.

24. *The Photographic Journal* 3:3, p. 118.

25. See *World Encyclopedia of Mythology*, foreword by Rex Warner (New York: Galahad Books, 1975), p. 11.

26. Joseph Campbell, *The Hero with a Thousand*

*Faces*, Bollingen Series XVII (Princeton, N.J.: Princeton University Press, 1973), p. 19.

27. "Some Humanistic Considerations of Photography," p. 167.

28. *Contemporary Photographer*, Carl Chiarenza, ed., 5:4 (1967), not paginated.

29. Etienne Gilson, *Painting and Reality* (Cleveland and New York: World Publishing Co., Meridian Books, 1965), "Painters and the Talking World," p. 211.

30. "Notes on Uelsmann's Invented World," *Infinity*, Charles Reynolds, ed., 16:2 (February 1967), p. 33.

31. *The Village Voice*, September 26, 1968, p. 20.

32. "Wynn Bullock/Tracing the Roots of Man in Nature," *Modern Photography* 34:5 (May 1970), p. 89.

33. From original draft (January 1971) of the lecture later published in *The Photographic Journal* (April 1971).

34. In *Darkroom*, Eleanor Lewis, ed., p. 180.

35. Gilson, *Painting and Reality*, pp. 171, 176.

36. Letter to Michael Hoffman (June 1978) with copy to the author, concerning proposed publication unrelated to this monograph.

37. Szarkowski, *Mirrors and Windows: American Photography Since 1960* (New York: The Museum of Modern Art, 1978), p. 23.

38. *The New York Times*, January 2, 1981.

39. *Artweek* (May 31, 1980), review of exhibition catalogue by Joan Murray for Exhibition at Chicago Center for Contemporary Photography, 1980. Contains essay by the author drawn from notes for current monograph.

# Chronology

## *Jerry Norman Uelsmann*

**1934**
Born in Detroit, Michigan. Attends public schools and in high school (at age fourteen) develops interest in photography.

**1953–1960**
Attends Rochester Institute of Technology (B.F.A., M.A.) and Indiana University (M.F.A.). Inspired and influenced by teachers Minor White, Ralph Hattersley, and Henry Holmes Smith.

**1960–1966**
Joins faculty of Department of Art, University of Florida, as Instructor of Art, at invitation of Van Deren Coke. Founding member and elected to Board of Directors of the National Society for Photographic Education.

**1967–1970**
One-man exhibition at the Museum of Modern Art, New York. Receives Guggenheim Fellowship. Conducts workshops and delivers lectures throughout the United States at major universities and art institutions. Promoted to Professor of Art, University of Florida. Cited for outstanding contributions to photography by the American Society of Magazine Photographers. Portfolio of work presented in major U.S. and European publications. First retrospective exhibition, at the Philadelphia Museum of Art. Complete issue of *Aperture* (15:4) devoted to his work, with essay by Peter C. Bunnell.

**1971–1973**
Invited to deliver fourth Bertram Cox Memorial Lecture, entitled "Some Humanistic Considerations of Photography," at the Royal Photographic Society, London. Continues to lecture and give workshops throughout United States and Europe. Receives National Endowment for the Arts

Fellowship. Limited-edition portfolio of photographs issued by the Witkin Gallery, New York. Made Fellow of Royal Photographic Society of Great Britain. Participates as one of several featured artists at fourth Rencontres Internationales de la Photographie in Arles, France.

**1974–1977**
Appointed Graduate Research Professor, University of Florida. Receives Certificate of Merit from the Society of Publication Designers and Certificate of Excellence from American Institute of Graphic Arts, both for contributions to *The New York Times*. Publication of first monograph on his work, *Silver Meditations*, Introduction by Peter C. Bunnell. Work included in international exhibitions in London, Paris, Montreal, and Zagreb. One-man exhibitions at more than a half-dozen commercial galleries and at an equal number of major museums and art centers, including a 225-print retrospective at the San Francisco Museum of Modern Art.

**1978–1981**
Receives Bronze Medal at 19th Zagreb Salon, International Exhibition of Photography held in Yugoslavia. Included in major national and international exhibitions, including *Mirrors and Windows* (Museum of Modern Art, New York) and group shows in Holland, Canada, Australia, and Japan. Honored as Visiting Professor, Nihon University, College of Art, Tokyo. Named one of top ten most collected photographers, preceded only by Ansel Adams, Edward Weston, Walker Evans, and Lewis Hine, in a report by *American Photographer*.

# Selected Bibliography

**1964**
Smith, Henry Holmes. "The Photography of Jerry N. Uelsmann." *Contemporary Photographer* 5:1, pp. 47–48.

**1965**
Kinzer, H. M. "Jerry Uelsmann: '. . . involved with the celebration of life'." *Popular Photography* 57:5 (November), pp. 136–144, 177–181.

**1967**
Parker, William. "Notes on Uelsmann's Invented World." *Infinity* 16:2 (February), pp. 4–13, 32–33.

Lyons, Nathan, ed. *The Persistence of Vision.* New York: Horizon Press, in conjunction with International Museum of Photography at George Eastman House, n.p.

**1968**
Parker, William. "Uelsmann's Unitary Reality." *Aperture* 13:3, n.p.

**1969**
Bunnell, Peter C. "Photography as Print-making." *Artist's Proof.* Fritz Eichenberg, ed., pp. 24–40. New York: Pratt Graphics Center.

**1970**
Bunnell, Peter C. "Jerry N. Uelsmann." *Aperture* 15:4, n.p.

Klein, Jean A. *Histoire de la Photographie,* p. 117. Paris: Presses Universitaires de France.

Mason, Robert G., ed. "The Impact of Multiple Images," *The Print,* pp. 214–219. New York: Time-Life Books.

Ward, John L. *The Criticism of Photography as Art: The Photographs of Jerry Uelsmann.* Gainesville: University of Florida Press.

**1971**
*Arts et Techniques Graphiques* 81, Club Photographique de Paris, pp. 8–9.

Coleman, A. D. "He Captures Dreams, Visions, Hallucinations." *The New York Times* (January 3), p. D14.

———. "Latent Image." *The Village Voice* (February 18), p. 16.

Deschin, Jacob. "What They're Teaching Today." *35mm Photography* (Winter), pp. 42–47.

Rice, Leland. "Ideas and Jerry Uelsmann." *Artweek* 2:19 (May 8), p. 7.

**1972**
Brettell, Richard. "Four Directions in Modern Photography: Paul Caponigro, John T. Hill, Jerry N. Uelsmann, Bruce Davidson." Preface by Alan Shestack. Yale University Art Gallery, n.p. (catalogue).

Coleman, A. D. "Latent Image." *The Village Voice* (April 20), p. 31.

Gassan, Arnold. *A Chronology of Photography,* pp. 41, 212, 209. Athens, Ohio: Handbook Company.

Thornton, Gene. "Uelsmann: Does He See Ghosts?" *The New York Times* (April 16), p. D23.

**1973**
*Nouveau Photo Cinema* 15 (July–August), pp. 22–30, 76.

**1974**
Doty, Robert, ed. *Photography in America,* pp. 9, 21. Published for the Whitney Museum of American Art. New York: Random House.

Gassan, Arnold. "Gros Plan." *France Photographie* 38 (November), pp. 17–24.

Gautrand, Jean-Claude. "Jerry N. Uelsmann." *Photo-Revue* (February), pp. 66–75.

*Photography Year 1974*, pp. 156–157. New York: Time-Life Books.

Swedlund, Charles. *Photography: A Handbook of History, Materials, and Processes*, p. 46. New York: Holt, Rinehart, and Winston.

**1975**
Bunnell, Peter C. *Silver Meditations*. Dobbs Ferry, New York: Morgan and Morgan.

Marie, Alain. "Jerry Uelsmann et la vision surréaliste." *Information and Documents*, pp. 20–23. D.L. 3e trim. Paris: American Services of Information and Cultural Relations.

**1976**
Brandt, Bill. *The Land*, p. 48. London: The Victoria and Albert Museum (exhibition catalogue).

**1977**
Lewis, Eleanor, ed. *Darkroom*, pp. 172–183. New York: Lustrum Press.

Thornton, Gene. *Masters of the Camera*, pp. 9, 25, 218–221. New York: Holt, Rinehart, and Winston.

**1978**
*Fotografi* 7/8 (July/August), pp. 51–55. Sweden.

*Progresso Fotografico* (March), pp. 62–63. Italy.

Szarkowski, John. *Mirrors and Windows: American Photography Since 1960*, pp. 34–35. New York: The Museum of Modern Art.

**1979**
Enyeart, James L. "Curator's Choice." *Photography Venezia '79* (Summer), UNESCO; p. 367 (exhibition catalogue).

Hugunin, James. "Tarnished Meditations: Some Thoughts on Jerry Uelsmann's Photographs." *Afterimage* 6:10 (May), pp. 8–11.

Peters, Susan Dodge. "The Inclusion of Medieval and Victorian Art in Jerry Uelsmann's Photographs: A Reading of Associations." *Image* 22:1 (March). International Museum of Photography at George Eastman House.

**1980**
Enyeart, James. L. "Spontaneous Mythology." *Jerry N. Uelsmann: Photographs from 1975–79*. Chicago Center for Contemporary Photography (exhibition catalogue).

**1981**
Kramer, Don Edward. "Florida's Jerry Uelsmann: The High Art of Creative Photography." *Art Voices* 4:4 (July–August), pp. 44–46.

## Articles and Major Statements by Jerry Uelsmann

**1962**
"New Talent USA." *Art in America*, 50:1, p. 49.

**1965**
"Heliographers." *Photography Annual 1965*, p. 197. New York: Ziff Davis Publishing Co.

**1967**
"Post-Visualization." *Florida Quarterly* 1 (Summer), pp. 82–89. Reprinted in *Creative Camera* 60 (June 1969), pp. 212–219, and in *Contemporary Photographer* 5:4 (1967). Excerpted in *Camera* 46 (January 1967), pp. 6–19.

**1970**

Mason, Robert G., and Norman Snyder, eds. "The Multiple Print," *The Camera*, p. 44. New York: Time-Life Books.

"Wynn Bullock/Tracing the Roots of Man in Nature." *Modern Photography* 34:5 (May) p. 89.

**1971**

Williams, Richard L., ed. "Challenging the Traditions," *The Art of Photography*, pp. 152–153. New York: Time-Life Books.

Fourth Bertram Cox Memorial Lecture: "Some Humanistic Considerations of Photography." *The Photographic Journal* 3:4 (April), pp. 165–182. London: The Royal Photographic Society.

**1972**

Parker, Fred R., ed. "Creativity is Contagious: A Second Look at the Creative Experience Workshop." *Untitled* 2/3, pp. 56, 58, 78.

**1973**

Kemp, Weston. *Photography for Visual Communicators*, p. 214. Englewood Cliffs, NJ: Prentice-Hall, Inc.

**1974**

"I Have Long Been Nourished by Enigma.". *Untitled* 7/8, pp. 47–57.

"Photography." *Newsweek* 84 (October), p. 68.

# Selected One-Man Exhibitions

**1967**
The Museum of Modern Art, New York

**1969**
Carl Siembab Gallery of Photography, Boston

**1970**
Philadelphia Museum of Art

International Museum of Photography at George Eastman House, Rochester

**1972**
The Witkin Gallery, New York

The Art Institute of Chicago

**1974**
American Cultural Center, Paris

The Photography Place, Berwyn, Pennsylvania

**1975**
Washington Gallery of Photography, Washington, D.C.

The Witkin Gallery, New York

**1976**
Déjà Vu Gallery, Toronto

Center for Creative Photography, University of Arizona, Tucson

**1977**
San Francisco Museum of Modern Art

The Witkin Gallery, New York

**1978**
Worcester Art Museum

Museum of Fine Arts, Santa Fe

Galerie Fiolet, Amsterdam

Nova Gallery, Vancouver

Photographers Gallery, Melbourne

**1979**
The Photography Place, Philadelphia

Atlanta Gallery of Photography

University Gallery, Nihon University, Tokyo

**1980**
The Chicago Center for Contemporary Photography and Columbia Gallery

# Public Collections

Bibliothèque Nationale, Paris

Center for Creative Photography, University of Arizona, Tucson

Emily Lowe Gallery, Hofstra University, Hempstead, New York

International Museum of Photography at George Eastman House, Rochester

Massachusetts Institute of Technology, Cambridge

National Gallery of Canada, Ottawa

Photographic Archives, University of Louisville

The Art Institute of Chicago

The Art Museum, Princeton University

The Museum of Modern Art, New York

The Royal Photographic Society of Great Britain, London

Worcester Art Museum

Yale University Art Gallery, New Haven

*Copyedited by Betsy Pitha*
*Designed by Howard I. Gralla*
*Composition in Monotype Walbaum by Michael & Winifred Bixler*
*Paper is Lustro Offset Enamel Gloss by S. D. Warren Co.*
*Single-impression printing by Murray Printing Co.*
*Duotone and color printing by Dynagraf Inc.*
*Bound by A. Horowitz and Son*